D1552177

THE LIFE AND LEGAL WRITINGS OF
HUGO GROTIUS

The Life
and
Legal Writings
of
HUGO
GROTIUS

by

Edward Dumbauld

CALVIN T. RYAN LIBRARY
KEARNEY STATE COLLEGE
KEARNEY, NEBRASKA

NORMAN

UNIVERSITY OF OKLAHOMA PRESS

BY EDWARD DUMBAULD

*Interim Measures of Protection in International Contro-
versies* (THE HAGUE, 1932)

Thomas Jefferson, American Tourist (NORMAN, 1946)

*The Declaration of Independence and What It Means
Today* (NORMAN, 1950)

The Political Writings of Thomas Jefferson (NEW YORK,
1955)

The Bill of Rights and What It Means Today (NORMAN,
1957)

The Constitution of the United States (NORMAN, 1964)

Sayings of Jesus (SCOTTDALE, 1967)

The Life and Legal Writings of Hugo Grotius (NORMAN,
1969)

STANDARD BOOK NUMBER: 8061–0848–7

LIBRARY OF CONGRESS CATALOG CARD NUMBER: 68–31373

COPYRIGHT 1969 BY THE UNIVERSITY OF OKLAHOMA PRESS,
PUBLISHING DIVISION OF THE UNIVERSITY. COMPOSED AND
PRINTED AT NORMAN, OKLAHOMA, U.S.A., BY THE UNIVERSITY
OF OKLAHOMA PRESS. FIRST EDITION.

TO THE MEMORY OF

CORNELIS VAN VOLLENHOVEN

W.J.M. VAN EYSINGA

AND

B.M. TELDERS

FELLOW-COUNTRYMEN OF GROTIUS
REVERED AND INSPIRING TEACHERS OF
THAT LAW
WHICH GOVERNS PEOPLES AND THEIR RULERS.

•

PREFACE

THE BRIEF ACCOUNT here presented of the eventful life of the world-renowned Dutch scholar Hugo Grotius seeks only to provide such biographical background as is needful for adequate study of his legal writings.

While Grotius was a prolific writer in many other fields, he was by profession a lawyer. He later served as public official and diplomat. He is best known, to be sure, as the "father of international law," by reason of the widespread influence of his famous treatise *De Jure Belli ac Pacis* (*On the Law of War and Peace*) published at Paris in 1625. Generations of statesmen and diplomats have cited that celebrated work. It was frequently consulted by the founding fathers of the nascent American nation, including, among others, John Adams, Thomas Jefferson, James Madison, James Wilson, and John Marshall.

An adequate up-to-date biography of Grotius is lacking. The diffuse two-volume work of Brandt and van Cattenburgh, published in 1727, constitutes the standard Dutch source.

The best modern treatment is the little book by the late Professor van Eysinga of Leyden published in 1945 on the occasion of the three-hundredth anniversary of the death of Grotius. (This is available also in a German translation.) Only those who are themselves familiar with the field can appreciate the enormous erudition crystallized by Judge van Eysinga in this slender volume of less than 150 pages. Much available material is also to be found in the writings of the late Professor van Vollenhoven of Leyden, whose death in 1933 prevented preparation of the biography of Grotius which he had planned.

In English the only biographical works are those of Vreeland and Knight, published in 1917 and 1925 respectively.

Likewise, the literature devoted to juristic analysis of the legal writings of Grotius is scant. In this area, the contributions of Professor Basdevant of the University of Paris (later President Judge of the International Court of Justice), as well as those of van Vollenhoven and van Eysinga, are outstanding.

The present study discusses the five law treatises which (except for a number of opinions advising clients written in the course of his professional practice) constitute the entire corpus of legal writings by Grotius.

My book is the result of combining and revising material contained in a series of articles which have appeared over a number of years in the Emory University *Journal of Public Law*, to which grateful acknowledgement is made for permission to reprint material published there. It was Thomas W. Christopher, formerly professor of law at Emory University, now dean of the law school at the University of New Mexico, who first suggested that it would be useful to bring these articles together into a unified comprehensive study of the celebrated Dutch jurist.

For the illustrations I am indebted to Dr. B. L. Meulenbroek of the Grotius Institute at The Hague. The engravings of Loevestein Castle are from his own private collection.

It is my wish and hope that this volume will serve to familiarize English-speaking lawyers, especially those who are active in the realm of international affairs, with the important contributions made by Grotius to the establishment of the rule of law as an ecumenical phenomenon.

Like the judicious Hooker, Grotius proclaimed that of the law no less can be acknowledged than this, that her voice is the harmony of the world, and that all things in heaven and in earth do her homage, the very least as feeling her care and the greatest as not exempted from her power.

EDWARD DUMBAULD

Pittsburgh, Pennsylvania
May 15, 1969

CONTENTS

ILLUSTRATIONS

PART ONE

LIFE OF GROTIUS

Studious Years

Hugo Grotius (or Huigh de Groot, as he was called in the tongue of his native Netherlands) was born in the colorful city of Delft on Easter day, April 10, 1583, at about seven o'clock in the evening. The dwelling of his father, Jan de Groot, stood on the Oude Langedijk.[1] The elder de Groot served four years as *burgemeester* of the city, and as curator of the University of Leyden from 1594 to 1617. He died in 1640 at an advanced age. Hugo's uncle, Cornelis de Groot,[2] was a professor of law at the celebrated university, founded in 1575 by William the Silent of Orange to reward the steadfast fidelity and bravery of the starving citizens of Leyden who refused to surrender to the Spaniards when the city was besieged in 1574.[3]

[1] Anne Berendsen, *Verborgenheden uit het oude Delft*, 63.

[2] On Cornelis de Groot, see W. S. M. Knight, *The Life and Works of Hugo Grotius*, 10–16 [hereinafter cited as Knight]. According to Berendsen, Jan de Groot lived 1554–1640; Hugo's brother Willem, 1582–1662; his wife Marie, 1590–1652.

[3] John L. Motley, *The Rise of the Dutch Republic*, II, 624–27; Robert J. Fruin, *The Siege and Relief of Leyden in 1574*, 140. During the siege the courageous *burgemeester* Pieter van der Werff had vigorously encouraged the spirit of resistance, especially by a memorable address in which he declared his willingness to die but his refusal to surrender the city while he lived. On October 3, 1574, a boy reconnoitering in the Spanish camp found that the enemy troops had withdrawn, leaving behind some scraps of *hutspot* (a mixture containing carrots and potatoes). Since then it has been the custom of the

3

It was therefore natural that the young Grotius, a prodigy who had composed Latin verses at eight years of age, should begin his studies at the University on August 3, 1594, when he was eleven years old.[4]

Doubtless then as now Leyden was a delightful seat of learning. The charm of the place has well been described by an English writer: "Leyden justifies one's dreams —here is the realization of . . . visions of scholarly peace . . . : the serenity of green trees, of ancient buildings, of tranquil water; sunlight falling through long afternoons into quiet squares, where in still rooms men write or muse; the atmosphere of elegant learning as a palimpsest on the atmosphere of fierce . . . heroic deeds."[5]

At fifteen years of age, Grotius received the doctorate, on May 5, 1598, at the University of Orleans, having accompanied Johan van Oldenbarnevelt to France on a diplomatic mission. It was on this occasion that the French King, Henri IV, greeted Grotius as "the miracle of Holland."

His first scholarly publication was an edition of Martianus Capella in 1599. Two years later his first tragedy *Adamus*

---

inhabitants of Leyden to partake of *hutspot* every year, upon the anniversary of the end of the siege, in commemoration of that event. Offered a choice between exemption from taxation for a certain period, or the establishment of a university, Leyden chose the university.

[4] Knight, 27–30. Grotius remained three years at the University.

[5] Marjorie Bowen, *The Netherlands Display'd*, 59. Regarding the courageous closing of the University during World War II when the Nazi invaders dismissed the illustrous professor E. M. Meiers, see R. P. Cleveringa, "B. M. Telders † 6 April 1945," *De Gids*, Vol. CVIII, No. 11 (Nov., 1945), 4–67, and Eelco N. van Kleffens, *Juggernaut over Holland*, 177–78.

Exul appeared as the chief item in a volume of religious verse entitled *Sacra*. Other writings in later years included poems, dramas, histories, and many works on theology and Biblical studies.

Law Practice

The young Grotius would doubtless have been happy to continue scholarly pursuits in the field of letters, but his father wished him to be a lawyer. On December 13, 1599, he was admitted to practice before the *Hof van Holland*, and two days later before the *Hooge Raad*.[6]

While he was practicing law at The Hague, Grotius wrote (during the last months of 1604 and the first of 1605) his first noteworthy legal treatise, on the law of prize (*De Jure Praedae*). As will be seen later, however, this work was not published until the nineteenth century, when the manuscript accidentally came to light. It was undertaken in the interest of the East India Company.

Another work of this period which was not published until the nineteenth century (a fragment only having survived) was his *Parallelon Rerumpublicarum* or *De Moribus ingenioque populorum Atheniensium, Romanorum, Batavorum*. Written in 1601 or 1602, this was a comparison of the national customs and characteristics of the Greek, Roman, and Dutch peoples. Since it emphasized the importance of good faith in dealings among nations, it is considered as the earliest work of Grotius on the subject of international law.[7]

[6] Hamilton Vreeland, *Hugo Grotius*, 26 [hereinafter cited as Vreeland].

[7] Willem J. M. van Eysinga, *Huigh de Groot, Een Schets*, 23, 26–28 [hereinafter cited as *Schets*]. See p. 72, below.

Public Servant of Holland

On November 12, 1607, a new phase in Grotius' career began. He was appointed *Advocaat-Fiscaal* for the court of Holland, Zeeland, and West-Friesland. This position combined the duties of prosecutor in criminal cases with oversight of the state's property interests.[8] His experience in this office left its mark on the masterpieces of legal writing which Grotius later produced.

On July 17, 1608, Grotius married Marie van Reigersberch. Four sons and three daughters were born of this union.[9] His heroic helpmeet (*heroina conjunx*) possessed the noble qualities ascribed to Dutch women by Grotius in his *Parallelon Rerumpublicarum*.[10] Her courage and devotion were later immortalized when she contrived her husband's famous escape on March 22, 1621, in a bookchest from the castle of Loevestein where he was imprisoned under a life sentence for a political offense.[11]

Further official advancement came to Grotius when on March 4, 1613, he accepted appointment as pensionary of

[8] Vreeland, 49–50; Knight, 76–78; *Schets*, 37–39.

[9] One son and two daughters died young. The behavior of his sons Cornelis, Pieter, and Dirk displeased Grotius, and he did not wish to have to rely on them to publish his posthumous writings. *Schets*, 42, 130; Knight, 113. See p. 158, below.

[10] *Schets*, 40.

[11] See p. 13, below.

the city of Rotterdam (an office formerly held by van Oldenbarnevelt himself) which carried with it a seat in the States-General of Holland and later in the States-General of the United Netherlands.[12] This position brought Grotius into politics. Five years later he became a victim of the tumultuous religious controversies which were a part of Dutch politics in that era.[13]

[12] Vreeland, 62–63; *Schets*, 50.
[13] *Schets*, 52, 61, 64–70; Vreeland, 68–84.

Imprisonment and Exile

In the struggle that raged between the Calvinists and Arminians over predestination and similar disputed points of theology, Grotius was aligned with the Arminians. He had been a pupil of Arminius at Leyden. He was never a Calvinist.[14] As *Advocaat-Fiscaal* he held the second highest office in Holland under the Arminian party. In 1617 he had become a member of the Committee of Councillors (*College van Gecommitteerde Raden*) which, with the *Landsadvocaat*, Johan van Oldenbarnevelt, conducted the day-to-day administration of the public business of the province of Holland.

A state function of the utmost importance at that time was the regulation of matters pertaining to religion. Under the loose federation established by the Union of Utrecht in 1579, each province had autonomy in church affairs. But although Holland was one of the largest and most powerful of the provinces, Holland and Utrecht were the only provinces controlled by the Arminians. The Calvinists constituted the majority in the United Netherlands as a whole. They were supported by Prince Maurits, and sought to advance their cause through action by the

[14] Joachim Schlüter, *Die Theologie des Hugo Grotius,* 108–109. Cornelia W. Roldanus, "De Groot als theoloog," *De Gids,* Vol. CVIII, No. 12 (Dec., 1945), 106. The Arminian creed was somewhat similar to that of High-Church Anglicans.

central government. They called for a nationwide synod to decide the disputed questions of doctrine. On November 11, 1617, the States-General decided to convoke the famous Synod of Dort, which met a year later.[15] Meanwhile the States of Holland had on August 3, 1617, adopted the so-called drastic resolution (*scherpe resolutie*), drafted by van Oldenbarnevelt, opposing a national synod and authorizing the cities to call out the militia (*waardgelders*) to preserve order.

Thus the doctrinal difference over predestination and similar matters became a constitutional conflict between the local and the central governments. Holland was arrayed against the Union. The latter was personified in Prince Maurits, who commanded the army and was backed by the authority of the States-General. The local militia upon whom the Arminian-controlled provinces relied was quickly demobilized and dispersed at the command of the Prince.

An unexpected Calvinist *coup d'état* proved fatal to the Arminian cause. On August 29, 1618, when Grotius entered the Binnenhof at The Hague to attend a meeting of the Committee of Councillors of Holland, he was notified by the doorkeeper to proceed to the apartments of the Prince where he would find van Oldenbarnevelt. There he was made prisoner by Captain of the Guard Pieter van der Meulen on behalf of the States-General. Rombout Hoogerbeets, pensionary of Leyden, and Johan van Oldenbarnevelt were also imprisoned.

Disregarding the usual judicial organization, the States-General set up a special tribunal of twenty-four judges to try the three political prisoners. This court on May 13, 1619,

15 On the Synod of Dort, see Willem J. M. van Eysinga, *Sparsa Collecta*, 290–323.

condemned van Oldenbarnevelt to death. Five days later Grotius was sentenced to life imprisonment in the castle of Loevestein, as was Hoogerbeets. Grotius regarded his trial as a nullity from the legal standpoint and denied the jurisdiction of the States-General, claiming that he was responsible only to his own province, Holland, under which he held office and which had authorized all the acts he had committed. The tribunal did not at first specify in its sentence the crime of which the three prisoners were found guilty, but later, on June 6, 1620, a supplemental judgment (*Verklaringe*) defined the charge as treason (*laesa majestas*).

Grotius had been imprisoned in the Binnenhof during the trial, but on June 6, 1619, his confinement began at Loevestein. He remained there not quite two years. Thanks to the intrepidity of his alert and stouthearted wife, he was able to escape. Hidden in his book-chest,[16] he was carried out of the castle on March 22, 1621, by the very soldiers set to guard him. The precious load, accompanied by the brave and resourceful servant girl Elsje van Houweningen, was safely delivered after a two-mile journey by water to the house of a friendly merchant at Gorcum.[17] After emerging from the chest, Grotius then made his way in disguise to Antwerp, and later proceeded to Paris. There he was cordially received by scholars of distinction and high official circles in France.[18]

[16] A book-chest which belonged to the family of Grotius and which may be the one in which he escaped can be seen, upon request, at the Prinsenhof museum in Delft. Berendsen, *Verborgenheden uit het oude Delft*, 63.

[17] Vreeland, 136–44.

[18] *Schets*, 85–86. King Louis XIII on February 26, 1622, granted Grotius a yearly pension of 3,600 gulden; but as a vain effort to encourage his submission to Rome, payments were often in arrears.

During his confinement at Loevestein, Grotius was productive as a writer. He composed his well-known treatise *On the Jurisprudence of Holland* during this period (although it was not published until 1631).[19] A popular treatise *On the Truth of the Christian Religion* was written at the same time.[20]

The religious controversies which had led to his imprisonment turned the mind of Grotius in his later years towards theology, scriptural interpretation, and church government.[21] Always a devout Christian believer, he cherished as he grew older a "burning desire" for the reunification of Christendom.[22] Among his theological works of note were *De Satisfactione Christi* (1617), *De Coenae Administratione* (1638), *Via ad Pacem Ecclesiasticam* (1642), and *Votum pro Pace Ecclesiastica* (1642). The first of these espoused what is known as the "governmental" theory of the atonement (regarding God as ruler, not as creditor as in

[19] See p. 123, below.

[20] This book has been compared to John Bunyan's *Pilgrim's Progress* by van Vollenhoven. It was written in simple Dutch verse, and especially intended for sailors. Cornelis van Vollenhoven, *Verspreide Geschriften*, I, 370 [hereinafter cited as *Writings*]; *Schets*, 77–79. The book had perhaps more readers even than *The Law of War and Peace*. The Latin version published in 1627 and the Dutch version issued five years earlier account for 157 items in the bibliography of Grotius by Jacob ter Meulen and P. J. J. Diermanse, while for *De Jure Belli ac Pacis* there are only 114.

[21] Knight, 245–66.

[22] "De brandende begeerte van Mr. Huigh de Groot (1583–1645)," in Berendsen, *Verborgenheden uit het oude Delft*, 61–76. In September, 1641, he wrote to his brother Willem: "Ik heb met een brandende begeerte door mijn geheele leven getracht naar de bevrediging der Christenen wereld." *Ibid.*, 63. But it was after his experience of strife between Calvinists and Arminians that he turned toward theological studies. *Schets*, 22–23, 29–30, 54, 61–64, 76–79, 130–37. See also Knight, 277–84.

14

Anselm's theory). This doctrine was regarded by Calvinists as Socinian. It influenced Wesley and Jonathan Edwards.[23] In his treatise on the administration of the Eucharist, Grotius held that laymen might validly administer that sacrament in the absence of an ordained clergyman.[24] In his desire for ecclesiastical peace and for unity of Christendom, Grotius was willing to make such great concessions in order to restore union with Rome that he was attacked as a papist.[25] His strongly Erastian views regarding the relations of church and state, holding that paramount authority belongs to the secular power, were voiced in his *De Imperio Summarum Potestatum circa Sacra* written in 1614 but published posthumously in 1647.[26] A curious item among the minor works of Grotius, with Biblical overtones, is a dissertation *On the Origin of the Native Races of America*.[27]

Soon after his arrival in Paris, Grotius began work on his *Apologeticus*, which may be regarded as a major legal

[23] Knight, 269–70.

[24] Schlüter, *Die Theologie des Hugo Grotius*, 113; Knight, 282.

[25] For the controversy arising from publication of Laurentius, *Hugo Grotius Papizans*, in 1642, see ter Meulen and Diermanse, *Bibliographie de Grotius*, 600; Knight, 282; and Schlüter, *Die Theologie des Hugo Grotius*, 111.

[26] *Writings*, I, 392; *Schets*, 61–62; Knight, 167–284. An English translation believed to be by Clement Barksdale was published in 1651 with the title *Of the Authority of the Highest Powers about Sacred Things. Or the Right of the State in the Church, put into English by C. B.* This book generalized the view taken, with respect to the action of the States of Holland, by Grotius in his *Ordinum Hollandiae ac Westfrisiae Pietas . . . vindicata* published in 1613.

[27] Edinburgh, privately printed, 1884. *De Origine gentium Americanarum dissertatio* was published in Paris in 1642. Herbert P. Wright, "Some Lesser Known Works of Hugo Grotius," *Bibliotheca Visseriana*, Vol. VII (1928), 218.

treatise on Dutch public law.[28] It arose from a suggestion of Pierre Jeannin, one of the French king's ministers with whom the exiled Dutch jurist was intimately associated in Paris, that Grotius should write, while the events were fresh in his mind, a defense of his own good name and of the legality of the conduct in which he had engaged as an official of the government of Holland.[29] Grotius insisted that everything which he had done for which he had been imprisoned was done as agent of the government of Holland, in the due exercise of the constitutional powers possessed by that government, and that the central government had no lawful power or jurisdiction to try or condemn him.

Another major event of his Paris years was publication by Grotius in 1625 of his world-famous treatise *On the Law of War and Peace* which won for him the designation "father of international law."[30]

Grotius remained in exile in Paris until 1631. He then thought it safe to return to Holland where he practiced law in Amsterdam for three months. But he was again obliged to flee, leaving for Hamburg on April 17, 1632. The three years spent in Germany were the most unfruitful of his life.[31] In 1634 he was appointed ambassador of Sweden to France. He held this post until the middle of March, 1645, when he received his letter of recall from Queen Christina,

[28] *Schets*, 91–92. See p. 83, below.

[29] Caspar Brandt and Adriaan van Cattenburgh, *Historie*, I, 280. By Holland is meant, of course, not the whole United Netherlands, but the Province of Holland and West Friesland, of which Grotius was a high official at the time of his arrest in 1618.

[30] See p. 57, below.

[31] *Writings*, I, 485, 582; *Schets*, 99–105.

dated December 30, 1644. This recall was in accord with
the views of Grotius regarding the dignity of the government
he served, for the French king had withdrawn his diplomatic
representative at Stockholm since his dealings with Sweden
could be more conveniently conducted by his ambassador
in Germany.[32]

Grotius wished to continue his career as a diplomat, and
he particularly wished to take part in the peace conference
at Osnabrück. At Stockholm he received honors and gifts
at the hands of the Queen, but nothing was done about an
appointment to another post. Instead it was suggested that
he bring his family to live in Sweden. Concluding that the
Swedish government had no plans for his further service
abroad, Grotius decided to rejoin his wife as promptly as
possible. He sailed for Lübeck on August 13, 1645, but was
obliged to land eight days later on the eastern coast of
Pomerania on account of a severe storm at sea in which
the vessel lost one of its masts.

Pushing forward by wagon, he reached Rostock, in Meck-
lenburg, but was unable to proceed farther. Two of the six
servants who accompanied him carried him to bed in the
house of Catherine Ballmann, a widow, where he received
medical attention, and also Christian consolation from Pas-

[32] Knight, 287; *Schets*, 126. Besides the reasons officially given,
there may have been others. *Schets*, 126. One view is that Oxen-
stierna kept Grotius in Paris because Richelieu wished his recall, so that
after the Cardinal's death there was no point in his remaining there.
Immersed in scholarly pursuits, he may have been of slight practical
service to his sovereign. Jules Basdevant, "Crotius," in *Les Fondateurs
du Droit International*, 151. An apocryphal anecdote is told that at
a reception for ambassadors by the French king, Grotius neglected
his diplomatic amenities and stood aside in a window niche perusing
an interesting edition of the New Testament. Dumbauld, "Some Modern Misunderstandings of Grotius," 63.

tor Quistorp. Death came on the night of August 28, 1645.[33]
His last words were: "By undertaking many things, I have
accomplished nothing."[34]

An English writer has fittingly declared that "the Netherlands were to the seventeenth what the England of the
Revolution was to the eighteenth and early nineteenth centuries, a working model of free institutions, and the centre
of light for the rest of Europe. . . . The Dutch were placed
'in the very Thermopylae of the universe.' But for their
resistance it is almost certain that European liberty would
have succumbed to the universal aggression of Spain. . . .
In the days of their triumph the Netherlands became the
University of Europe."[35] Foremost among the jurists who

[33] *Writings*, I, 380–82; *Schets*, 126, 139; Alphonse Rivier, "La
Mort de Grotius," *Revue de Droit international et de Législation
comparée*, Vol. XIX, No. 1 (1887), 97.

[34] Knight, 289. According to another and perhaps more probable
account, his last words were: "I hear your voice well, but I under-
stand with difficulty what you say." Vreeland, 233.

[35] John N. Figgis, *Studies of Political Thought from Gerson to
Grotius*, 167, 170. "When Holland had trained this country to keep
alight the torch of liberty and enlightment, the historical mission was
over, and she sank into a second-rate power." *Ibid.*, 172. The flame
later spread to the New World. To Americans in 1776 the "glorious
revolution" of 1688 in England was a vivid reality and a heartening
precedent. Dumbauld, *The Declaration of Independence and What
It Means Today*, 21–22. The Dutch example was also in their minds.
The Dutch people likewise noted the resemblance and supported
the American cause. Friedrich Edler, *The Dutch Republic and the
American Revolution*, 15; J.C. Westermann, *The Netherlands and
the United States*, 2–3; F. W. van Wijk, *De republiek en Amerika*,
256. For a colorful account of the glory of the Dutch nation in the
seventeenth century and of the place of Grotius therein, see Conrad
Busken-Huet, *Het Land van Rembrand*, 67–91 of part 1, and 23–30
and 109–41 of part 2; and G. S. Overdiep, "Hugo de Groot en onze
nationale renaissance," *De Gids*, Vol. CIII–1, No. 2 (Feb., 1939),
188–208.

added in that era to the luster of the Netherlands stands Hugo Grotius. His mortal remains repose at Delft in the same church with those of another great national hero, William the Silent.[36] But his spirit still summons mankind to desist from lawless and unjust resort to warfare, and bids the nations of the world instead to respect and enforce the precepts of that system of law which prescribes the legal rights and duties of peoples and their rulers.[37]

[36] The plan for a tomb by Rombout Verhulst not having been realized, there stands in the Nieuwe Kerk a simple monument by H. von Zwoll, erected by the Grotius family in 1781. Berendsen, *Verborgenheden uit het oude Delft*, 76. The nations came to pay homage at this shrine on April 10, 1883, the three-hundredth anniversary of the birth of Grotius, and again three years later when a bronze statue was erected in front of the church to his memory. On July 4, 1899, the American delegation to the Hague Peace Conference laid a wreath at the tomb on behalf of the United States. Vreeland, 239. Subsequently on August 25, 1931, the American member of the Permanent Court of International Justice, Judge Frank B. Kellogg, made the speech of presentation on behalf of the American Bar Association of a stained-glass window depicting incidents in the life of Grotius. Dumbauld, "The Place of the Lawyer in International Affairs," *Uniontown, Pa., Morning Herald* (Feb. 6, 1933).

[37] *Prolegomena* 1 in *De Jure Belli ac Pacis*: "jus illud, quod inter populos plures aut populorum rectores intercedit."

PART TWO

LEGAL WRITINGS OF GROTIUS

On the Law of Prize
De Jure Praedae

The publication in 1950 of an English translation of Hugo Grotius' *De Jure Praedae*[1] has enabled a larger circle of readers to realize how extensively[2] the Dutch jurist drew upon this lesser-known treatise when composing his world-famous *De Jure Belli ac Pacis*, which was published at Paris in 1625.[3]

While more than a hundred editions and translations of the *Law of War and Peace* have appeared,[4] the *Law of Prize* remained unpublished until 1868. In that year an excellent edition, in the original Latin, was issued by Dr.

[1] Grotius, *Commentary on the Law of Prize and Booty* [hereinafter cited as *L. P. B.*] (Williams and Zeydel's trans., 1950). The second volume of this Carnegie Endowment publication is a collotype reproduction of the manuscript.

[2] This indebtedness to the earlier work of 1604 was indicated by the eminent Dutch authority on Grotius, Cornelis van Vollenhoven, in his excellent study *The Framework of Grotius' Book De Iure Belli ac Pacis (1625)* [hereinafter cited as *Framework*]. See also van Vollenhoven, *Verspreide Geschriften*, I, 225–30; II, 416–18.

[3] Concerning the book of 1625, see p. 57, below.

[4] P. 59, below.

H. G. Hamaker.[5] The only translation into any modern language prior to the English version mentioned above was a Dutch translation in 1934.[6] Chapter XII of the book was brought out separately in 1609 under the title *Mare Liberum*[7] and won much acclaim during the controversy with England over freedom of the seas, a dispute in which the British pretensions were upheld by the learned and witty John Selden.[8]

The manuscript of *De Jure Praedae* came to light almost by accident in 1864 when the Dutch bookseller Martinus Nijhoff at The Hague offered it for sale with some other papers of the Cornets–de Groot family. It came to the attention of several professors of the University of Leyden and was purchased by the University. Professor Robert Fruin, a noted historian, persuaded Hamaker to undertake the task of editing it, and himself wrote an article, later translated into English, which has been the principal treatment of the subject available to students of international law.[9]

I.

In the first chapter of *De Jure Praedae*, Grotius explains the nature of his subject and outlines the order of treat-

[5] *De Jure Praedae Commentarius* [hereinafter cited as *D. J. P.*] (Hamaker's ed., 1868). I have used this edition and am responsible for the English translation of passages quoted. For the convenience of readers, however, I have added page references to the Williams and Zeydel translation wherever I cite *De Jure Praedae*.

[6] *Verhandeling over het Recht op buit* (Damsté's trans., 1934).

[7] Translated into English by Ralph van Deman Magoffin: *The Freedom of the Seas.*

[8] Selden's *Mare Clausum*, written in 1618, was published in 1635.

[9] Robert J. Fruin, "An Unpublished Work of Hugo Grotius's," *Bibliotheca Visseriana*, Vol. V (1925), 3–74. This is a translation of

ment. The question to be investigated is whether it is proper for the captors to receive as "prize" the proceeds of property captured from the enemy. As Grotius indicates, it is difficult for a foreigner to see why anyone should have any doubts; but certain shareholders, of Mennonite persuasion, in the East India Company had questioned the propriety of the practice. They even considered the formation of a competing company in France which would abstain from privateering and confine its activities to peaceful trading and purely commercial pursuits.

Grotius was drawn into the dispute in 1604 when as a young lawyer of twenty-one he was retained by the directors of the Amsterdam chamber of the East India Company to justify the practice of capturing enemy goods. Scholars now believe that Grotius was not employed as attorney for the Company in the prize court proceedings involving the *Catharina*, but that his work was intended, like that of a modern "public relations counselor," to influence public opinion.[10] The manuscript was completed in 1606 but was not published, probably because it was felt that under then-prevailing sentiment no such doctrinal justification

"Een Onuitgegeven Werk van Hugo De Groot," reprinted from *De Gids*, Vol. XXXII, No. 4 (Oct., 1868) in *Verspreide Geschriften*, Vol. III (1901), 367–445. See also Philip C. Molhuysen, "Over Grotius' De Jure Praedae Commentarius," *Bijdragen voor Vaderlandsche Geschiedenis en Oudheidkunde*, Vol. IV (1926), 275–82; and Willem J. M. van Eysinga, "Quelques Observations au Sujet du Mare Liberum et du De Iure Praedae de Grotius, *Grotiana*, Vol. IX (1942), 60.

[10] *Schets*, 23–24; Willem J. M. van Eysinga, "Het oudste bekende geschrift van de Groot over Volkenrecht," in *Mededeelingen der Nederlandsche Akademie van Wetenschappen, Afdeeling Letterkunde*, Nieuwe Reeks, Vol. IV, No. 11 (1941), 463–64; Molhuysen, "Grotius' De Jure Praedae," *loc. cit.*, 275, 276, 279–80.

was necessary. The growing wealth which was put into circulation as the result of Dutch maritime prowess doubtless proved more convincing to the thrifty populace than the conscientious scruples of the Mennonites against the use of armed force.

The particular case which had attracted widespread attention and which Grotius used as the basis of his book was the capture by Jacob van Heemskerck on February 25, 1603, of the *Catharina*, a richly laden Portuguese carack (a type of vessel) in the Strait of Singapore, which separates Sumatra from Malacca. Van Heemskerck was sailing in the service of a company which had merged with the East India Company, and on September 9, 1604, the captured vessel was condemned by the College of Admiralty, the Dutch court having jurisdiction of such matters. Following sale[11] the proceeds were ordered distributed, in the proportions prescribed by law, to the East India Company and to Admiral van Heemskerck and his men.

To satisfy the various types of doubts entertained by his countrymen, Grotius determined to treat the question of prize not only from the standpoint of whether it was legally justified (Chapters II–XIII), but also from the standpoint of whether it was honorable (Chapter XIV) and expedient (Chapter XV).

In discussing the legality of capturing enemy goods, Grotius emphasizes that the criterion is to be found not in

[11] The States of Holland, a third claimant, on September 1, 1604, relinquished their rights. A sale of perishable silks in the cargo had been held on August 15, 1604, before the judgment. The subsequent sale of china, lacquer work, and other curiosities began on September 21, 1604. Fruin, "An Unpublished Work of Hugo Grotius's," *loc. cit.*, 22, 23, 25, 28.

written codes of Roman law[12] but in natural reason, in "the whole law of war and peace."[13] He proceeds to enumerate in Chapters II–X what he calls *dogmatica,* his exposition of the legal principles applicable. In Chapter XI he marshals the *historica,* an account of the historical facts about Dutch traders in the Indies and the outrages endured by them in their conflicts with the Portuguese.

Applying the law to the facts, Grotius develops in Chapter XII (which, we have already noted, was published in 1609 at the request of the East India Company under the title *Mare Liberum*) his thesis of freedom of the seas[14] and the right of nations under international law to trade with one another.[15] From these principles it follows that the Dutch were justified in making war upon the Portu-

---

[12] Regarding the attitude of Grotius to Roman law generally, see van Eysinga, "Quelques Observations sur Grotius et le Droit Romain," *Grotiana.* Vol. X (1947), 18–28.

[13] "Nam illi quidem operam mihi ludere videntur, qui res non inter cives sed populos diversos gestas, idque non pace sed bello, ex scriptis duntaxat legibus dijudicant. [Baldus] sapienter docuit inter eos, qui supremam imperii potestatem sibi vindicant, si quid inciderit contentionis, non alium dari judicem, quem naturalem rationem, bonorum atque malorum arbitram. . . . Aliunde igitur quam ex legum Romanarum corpore petenda est praestabilis illa scientia, quam Cicero dicit consistere in foederibus, pactionibus, conditionibus populorum regum exterarumque nationum, in omni denique belli jure ac pacis." *D.J.P.,* 5–6; *L.P.B.,* 6. This quotation from Cicero's oration *Pro Balbo,* c. 6, § 15, may have suggested to Grotius the title of his famous treatise *De Jure Belli ac Pacis.* See also *Framework,* 158; and *D.J.P.,* 129; *L.P.B.,* 131, citing Livy, bk. 5, c. 27:"Sunt et belli sicut et pacis jura. . . ." See also van Vollenhoven, *Verspreide Geschriften,* I, 361.

[14] "The sea cannot be anyone's property." *D.J.P.,* 220, 222; *L.P.B.,* 232, 236.

[15] "Primum ergo illud positum sit jure gentium primario jubente, cujus ratio perpetua est et immutabilis, licere Batavis quibusvis cum gentibus negotiari." *D.P.J.,* 205; *L.P.B.,* 218. See also *D.J.P.,* 244; *L.P.B.,* 257.

guese, and hence in capturing their property as prize, because the Portuguese claimed a monopoly of trade with the Indies and interfered with the right of the Dutch to trade there.[16] The East India Company was thus entitled to its booty from the captured *Catharina.*

Grotius proceeds, in Chapter XIII, to confirm this conclusion (which he based in Chapter XII on the hypothesis that the Company was lawfully waging a private war on its own account to redress injuries and protect its legal rights) by showing that in reality the conflict was a public war, lawfully waged by authority of the sovereign States of Holland.[17] As an additional justification for the East India Company's rightful ownership of the booty captured, he adduces the grievances of the native states in the Indies themselves, whom the Dutch were bound to aid as allies.[18]

In the two concluding chapters, Grotius demonstrates that the capture of enemy property as prize is honorable and expedient, as well as lawful.

The book ends with an earnest prayer that the enemies of Holland may be overthrown:[19]

I beseech the immortal God, sole author and educator of this republic, Whom on account of His will we call the Best and on account of His power the Greatest, Whom it hath pleased to choose the Dutch above all others that through them He might show how feeble is every human greatness when measured against His

[16] D.J.P., 249, 266; L.P.B., 262, 281.
[17] D.J.P., 268, 270; L.P.B., 283, 285.
[18] D.J.P., 299; L.P.B., 314-16.
[19] D.J.P., 341. For another translation, see L.P.B., 365-66. Compare the broader vision of the prayer with which the *Law of War and Peace* concludes. Pp. 71-72, below.

might, and moreover to make known the glory of that people in the most remote regions of the world created by Him, humbly praying, first that He may give them such demeanor as befits the Christian name, lest their vices among pagan nations harm the true religion, next that He may confound the cruel counsels of our enemies, and that it be not His will that the innocent succumb to their ferocity, but that He may strike those down with disaster and slaughter, and raise up these with praise and glory; that He may hold in check the baleful fury of civil discord; that He may give sound judgment to the erring, and that to all He may give such wisdom that we may use and enjoy victory, which we recognize as the gift of heaven, with pure and thankful hearts.

The literary qualities of *De Jure Praedae* are remarkable. In arrangement and logical order, in cogency of argument, and in citation of authorities this work has few equals. It has rightly been called "a triumph of juristic art."[20] Moreover, the vigorous style of the young author is colorful and hearty. He abounds with patriotic fervor and passionate zeal for his countrymen, and describes in telling language their struggles for liberty against their Spanish oppressors and the injuries inflicted upon them by their Portuguese rivals for trade in the Indies.[21]

[20] "C'est le triomphe du raisonnement juridique." Basdevant, "Grotius," *loc. cit.*, 224.

[21] See especially Chapters XI, XII, and XV. For particularly eloquent passages, note the following: *D.J.P.*, 164–65, *L.P.B.*, 170; *D.J.P.*, 174–75, *L.P.B.*, 181–82; *D.J.P.*, 187–88, *L.P.B.*, 196 97; *D.J.P.*, 190–91, *L.P.B.*, 200; *D.J.P.*, 194–95, *L.P.B.*, 204–205; *D.J.P.*, 198, *L.P.B.*, 208; *D.J.P.*, 206, *L.P.B.*, 218; *D.J.P.*, 226, *L.P.B.*, 238–39; *D.J.P.*, 233, *L.P.B.*, 246; *D.J.P.*, 245, *L.P.B.*, 258; *D.J.P.*, 248–49, *L.P.B.*, 261–62; *D.J.P.*, 251, *L.P.B.*, 264; *D.J.P.*, 262, *L.P.B.*, 276; *D.J.P.*, 292, *L.P.B.*, 308; *D.J.P.*, 299, *L.P.B.*, 316; *D.J.P.*, 310–

This fiery nationalist ardor in the earlier work is perhaps the most striking contrast between it and the *Law of War and Peace*. Quite naturally, perhaps, a man two decades older, who had suffered imprisonment, escape, and exile, and who had been obliged by his countrymen to earn his bread as a courtier at the capital of another monarch, would not display in 1625 the same youthful convictions regarding the virtues of his native land's commercial policy and statecraft. The later book contains a fulsome dedication to King Louis XIII of France. In the earlier work Grotius criticized the errors into which jurists are likely to fall who so far forget the honorable nature of their profession as to seek to please the powerful with their opinions and who become sycophants to the throne.

In *De Jure Praedae*, as Fruin observes, Grotius thought of himself as a citizen of a republic which had recently won its liberty and independence by a successful rebellion; whereas when he wrote *De Jure Belli ac Pacis* he regarded his status as that of a ruler banished by an uprising against the legitimate government.[22]

In the earlier book, also, Grotius did not avoid references to current events as he did in the *Law of War and Peace*. In both works, however, he drew with great erudition upon

---

11, L.P.B., 329–30; D.J.P., 315, L.P.B. 335; D.J.P., 319, L.P.B., 340; D.J.P., 329, L.P.B., 352; D.J.P., 331–32, L.P.B., 355; D.J.P., 338, L.P.B., 362; D.J.P., 341, L.P.B., 365–66.

22 See p. 65, below; Fruin, "An Unpublished Work of Hugo Grotius's," *loc. cit.*, 59. For passages strongly upholding established authority, see D.J.P., 37, 79; L.P.B., 37, 79. For the right of rebellion, see D.J.P., 283, L.P.B., 299. See also van Vollenhoven, V*erspreide Geschriften*, I, 360; *Schets*, 30; D.J.P., 233; L.P.B., 246–47: ". . . quod sane jurisconsultis nimium est frequens, cum sanctae professionis auctoritatem non ad rationes et leges, sed ad gratiam conferunt potentiorum."

classical antiquity and Biblical writings for his illustrations and authorities.[23]

In another respect, also, a difference is observable between the earlier and the later work. Resort to war as an equivalent for judicial process was viewed by the younger Grotius more zestfully than in 1625. In the *Law of War and Peace* the author was more disposed to discourage warfare, and he dwelt with eloquent dismay upon the shameful license and lawlessness which he beheld throughout the Christian world of his day.[24]

Yet the fundamental theme of the two treatises is the same: that nations have legal rights and duties and that war is a law-enforcement procedure, akin to judicial remedies, to be employed to punish and redress violations of such rights and disregard of such duties.[25] Likewise there is no substantial difference in the system of legal analysis and definitions used by Grotius, in his treatment of international law topics, or in his philosophy of divine and natural law.[26] This will appear clearly upon analyzing Chapter II, in which Grotius defines the general legal concepts employed throughout the book, and Chapters III–X, which contain his demonstration of the lawfulness of war under certain conditions and the lawfulness of prize as an incident thereto.

II.

At the beginning of his *dogmatica*, in Chapter II, Grotius outlines the *prolegomena*, or basic axioms, which under-

[23] See p. 76, below.

[24] See pp. 68, 70, 75, below.

[25] See pp. 59–60, below.

[26] See pp. 73–75, below. But see *L.P.B.*, xxi, and Basdevant, "Grotius," *loc. cit.*, 232.

lie the arguments later to be advanced in the course of his discussion. Nine "rules" (*regulae*) and thirteen "laws" (*leges*) emerge as controlling principles of his legal philosophy.[27] The "rules" delineate the "sources of law" in the Grotian system.[28] The "laws" are fundamental standards of conduct having a concrete content.[29]

The nine "rules" defining what Grotius regards as law follow:

(1) What God makes known as His will is law.[30]

(2) What the consent of all men makes known as their will is law.[31]

(3) What each individual has made known as his will is law for him.[32]

(4) Whatever the commonwealth has made known as its will is law for the citizens collectively.[33]

[27] A list of these appears at L.P.B., 369–70.

[28] Regarding "sources of law" and the kindred doctrines of "constitutional" rules regarding the creation of law (*Grundnorm, Rechtserzeugungsverfahren,* and *Stufenbau*), see Gray, *The Nature and Sources of the Law*; Dumbauld, "The Place of Philosophy in International Law," *University of Pennsylvania Law Review,* Vol. LXXXIII, No. 5 (March, 1935), 590, 593, 606; Dumbauld, "Judicial Review and Popular Sovereignty," *University of Pennsylvania Law Review,* Vol. XCIX, No. 2 (Nov., 1950), 197, 198.

[29] They are "norms" prescribing rules to which human conduct *ought* to conform, not descriptive statements of actual behavior. Dumbauld, *Interim Measures of Protection in International Controversies,* 8.

[30] "Quod Deus se velle significarit, id jus est." *D.J.P.,* 7–8, L.P.B., 8.

[31] "Quod consensus hominum velle cunctos significaverit, id jus est." *D.J.P.,* 12; *L.P.B.,* 12.

[32] "Quod se quisque velle significaverit, id in eum jus est." *D.J.P.,* 18; *L.P.B.,* 18.

[33] "Quidquid respublica se velle significavit, id in cives universos jus est." *D.J.P.,* 23; *L.P.B.,* 23.

(5) Whatever the commonwealth has made known as its will is law for the citizens individually.[34]

(6) What the government has made known as its will is law for the citizens collectively.[35]

(7) What the government has made known as its will is law for the citizens individually.[36]

(8) Whatever all republics have made known as their will is law for all.[37]

(9) Priority in judging belongs to the commonwealth against which or against whose citizens a claim is asserted; but if that state defaults in its duty, then the commonwealth which itself (or whose citizen) is asserting the claim shall act as judge in that matter.[38]

This ninth rule is of basic importance to international law as expounded by Grotius. As we shall repeatedly have occasion to observe, Grotius both in *De Jure Praedae* and in *De Jure Belli ac Pacis* regards war as a mode of protecting rights and redressing wrongs, as an equivalent for judicial procedure in cases where such procedure is unavailable.[39]

---

[34] "Quidquid respublica se velle significavit, id inter cives singulos jus est." *D.J.P.*, 24; *L.P.B.*, 24.

[35] "Quod se magistratus velle significavit id in cives universos jus est." *D.J.P.*, 26; *L.P.B.*, 26.

[36] "Quod se magistratus velle significavit id in cives singulos jus est." *D.J.P.*, 26; *L.P.B.*, 26.

[37] "Quidquid omnes respublicae significarunt se velle, id in omnes jus est." *D.J.P.*, 26; *L.P.B.*, 26.

[38] "In judicando priores sint partes ejus reipublicae, unde cujusve a cive petitur. Quod si hujus officium cesset, tum respublica, quae ipsa cujusve civis petit, eam rem judicet." *D.J.P.*, 28; *L.P.B.*, 28.

[39] See p. 66, below. Compare with the quotation from *De Jure Belli ac Pacis* there cited the following from *De Jure Praedae*: "Totidem enim esse debent exsecutionum, quot sunt actionum genera, quod ad materiam attinet, quae in bello et judiciis eadem est." *D.J.P.*, 69; *L.P.B.*, 69. "Sicut autem in lite sic et in bello. . . ." *D.J.P.*, 70;

Such a case occurs when a dispute arises between sovereign states, over whom stands no overlord. Since it is not considered possible for the family of nations as a whole to come together to decide these controversies,[40] it is necessary to adopt the solution given in the ninth rule: let the defendant state first be called upon to judge, for it can do justice most easily; but if it denies justice, then the plaintiff state may act as judge. This power comes from the law of nature and is exercised whenever a state wages a just war.[41] A just war, Grotius observes further on in his treatise, is one which is waged to obtain a right.[42] War is an execution[43] by arms against an armed adversary.[44]

L.P.B., 69. ". . . non aliud in bello, aliud in forensi judicio statuendum est." D.J.P., 109; L.P.B., 111. "Naturaliter, sicuti diximus, juris quisque sui exsecutor est. . . ." D.J.P., 59; L.P.B., 60. "Jus autem et hic, sicut in re forensi, non omne ante exsecutionem nascitur. Est enim et hoc ipsum jus, id quod jus suum est exsequi: quod in praedae explicatione attigimus." D.J.P., 70; L.P.B., 69. See also notes 78, 96, and 120, below. The last-quoted sentence accords with the teachings of modern procedural science. Dumbauld, *Interim Measures of Protection in International Controversies*, 8, 18.

[40] "Nam sane supra rempublicam, quae est per se sufficiens multitudo, majus nullum imperium est." D.J.P., 28; L.P.B., 28. Arbitration is seemly, but not mandatory. D.J.P., 97; L.P.B., 98.

[41] "Nulla enim est reipublicae in rempublicam potestas ex conventione, sed ex natura, quae jus suum persequi unicuique permittit. . . . Nam quisquis justum bellum gerit, necesse est eatenus judex fiat adversarii. . . ." D.J.P., 29; L.P.B., 29. See pp. 45, 60, below.

[42] In Chapter IV: "Bellum autem justum idcirco est, quia ad juris adeptionem tendit." D.J.P., 43; L.P.B., 43. In Chapter VII: "Cum igitur bellum justum juris sit exsecutio. . . ." D.J.P., 66; L.P.B., 66. In Chapter VIII: "Bellum exsecutionem esse diximus." D.J.P., 85; L.P.B., 85. "Neque enim alio fine bella gerimus, quam ut jus nostrum victoria consequamur." D.J.P., 111; L.P.B., 112. In Chapter XII: "Verum belli finem esse diximus juris adeptionem. . . ." D.J.P., 263; L.P.B., 277.

[43] "Execution" here does not have its secondary sense of capital

Before proceeding to consider the questions treated in Chapter III and elsewhere in the *dogmatica* as to whether war (and prize) can ever be just, let us revert again to the preliminary axioms of Chapter II and glance at the thirteen "laws" which Grotius there lays down:

(1) It shall be lawful to protect life and ward off harmful things.[45]

(2) It shall be lawful to procure and retain those things that are useful for living.[46]

(3) Let no one do injury to another.[47]

(4) Let no one take possession of that which is possessed by another.[48]

(5) Wrongs done must be remedied.[49]

---

punishment, or the execution of a death sentence, but its more general meaning of the process by which physical power is brought into play to establish a situation of fact which corresponds to the requirements of law. A levy by the sheriff on a recalcitrant defendant's goods and chattels, or real estate, is the most common use of a writ of execution. Dumbauld, *Interim Measures of Protection in International Controversies,* 9–10; *D.J.P.,* 30; *L.P.B.,* 30: "Qua igitur actione jus ad eum, cui secundum regulas ac leges competit, perducitur, haec justa est: quae secus, injusta. Sed actiones ut ab animis incipiunt, ita desinunt in corporibus. Haec dicatur exsecutio." See also *D.J.P.,* 59; *L.P.B.,* 60.

[44] "Armata in armatum exsecutio bellum dicitur. . . ." *D.J.P.,* 30; *L.P.B.,* 30. ". . . nihil a forensi exsecutione bellum differt, nisi quod ob potentiam adversarii armis agendum est." *D.J.P.,* 128; *L.P.B.,* 130. "Bellum" is translated by van Vollenhoven as "armed coercion." *Framework,* 115, 120, 157.

[45] "Vitam tueri et declinare nocitura liceat." *D.J.P.,* 10; *L.P.B.,* 10.

[46] "Adjungere sibi quae ad vivendum sunt utilia eaque retinere liceat." *D.J.P.,* 10, *L.P.B.,* 10.

[47] "Ne quis alterum laedat." *D.J.P.,* 13; *L.P.B.,* 13.

[48] "Ne quis occupet alteri occupata." *D.J.P.,* 14; *L.P.B.,* 13.

[49] "Malefacta corrigenda." *D.J.P.,* 15; *L.P.B.,* 15.

(6) Benefits must be rewarded.[50]

(7) Individual citizens shall not only not injure, but shall protect, other citizens individually and collectively.[51]

(8) Citizens shall not only not steal what belongs to another or to the public, but shall contribute to individuals or the community those things that are necessary for them.[52]

(9) Let a citizen not execute his right against a citizen without a judicial judgment.[53]

(10) The government must in all things act for the good of the republic.[54]

(11) The republic must ratify whatever the government has done.[55]

(12) Neither the republic nor a citizen may execute its right against another republic or its citizen without a judicial judgment.[56]

[50] "Benefacta repensanda." *D.J.P.*, 15; *L.P.B.*, 15.

[51] "Ut singuli cives caeteros tum universos, tum singulos non modo non laederent, verum etiam tuerentur." *D.J.P.*, 21; *L.P.B.*, 21.

[52] "Ut cives non modo alter alteri privatim aut in commune possessa non eriperent, verum etiam singuli tum quae singulis, tum quae universis necessaria conferrent." *D.J.P.*, 21; *L.P.B.*, 21.

[53] "Ne civis adversus civem jus suum nisi judicio exsequatur." *D.J.P.*, 24; *L.P.B.*, 24. Grotius says that this law holds the first place among civil laws: "Atque adeo inter leges civiles prima est ista ad continendam societatem, quae judiciorum necessitatem facit. . . ." *D.J.P.*, 24; *L.P.B.*, 24. Judgment is defined as "the will of all directed toward individuals for the public good." "Voluntas universorum ad singulos directa boni publici intuitu *judicium* est. . . . est enim judicium lex ad factum singulare aptata."*D.J.P.*, 23, 24; see *L.P.B.*, 23, 24. Compare the definition of statute: "Voluntas universorum ad universos directa *lex* dicitur. . . ." *D.J.P.*, 22; *L.P.B.*, 22.

[54] "Ut magistratus omnia gerat e bono reipublicae." *D.J.P.*, 26; *L.P.B.*, 25.

[55] "Ut quidquid magistratus gessit respublica ratum habeat." *D.J.P.*, 26; *L.P.B.*, 25–26.

[56] "Ne respublica neu civis in alteram rempublicam alteriusve civem jus suum nisi judicio exsequatur." *D.J.P.*, 27; *L.P.B.*, 27.

(13) Let all laws be observed simultaneously where possible; where that cannot be done, let the worthier law prevail.[57]

Commenting on the thirteenth proposition, Grotius states that a law may be worthier in its origin or in its purpose. Thus by virtue of origin divine law prevails over human law, and human law over civil law.[58] By virtue of purpose, a law which concerns one's own good is to be preferred to that which concerns the good of someone else, and a law working a greater good to one working a lesser good.

III.

At this point it will be appropriate to define the various kinds of law which Grotius mentions.

"Primary law of nature" is the first category of which he speaks. This is law which derives its authority from the expressed will of God. What it commands or prohibits becomes just or unjust precisely because of the divine *ipse dixit*; it is not commanded or prohibited by God because of its inherent justness or unjustness per se. This category is identical with what Grotius in the *Law of War and Peace* more meaningfully calls "divine volitional law" (*jus divinum voluntarium*).[59]

[57] "Ut ubi simul observari possunt observentur: ubi id fieri non potest, tum potior sit quae est dignior." *D.J.P.*, 29; *L.P.B.*, 29. Grotius calls this "the law of all laws": "Legum igitur cunctarum quasi lex erit ista. . . ." *Ibid.*

[58] "Ex origine enim jus divinum juri humano, jus humanum juri civili praestat." *D.J.P.*, 29; *L.P.B.*, 29.

[59] "Jubere autem potestatis est. Prima potestas in omnia Dei . . . Dei voluntas non oraculis tantum et extraordinariis significationibus, sed vel maxime ex creantis intentione apparet. Inde enim *jus naturae est*." *D.J.P.*, 8; *L.P.B.*, 8. See p. 64, below.

"Secondary law of nature" or "primary law of nations" is the appellation which Grotius uses, following the terminology of his predecessors, to describe the rules of law which rest on reason. This category in the *Law of War and Peace* is called "law of nature" *simpliciter*. Universal agreement is evidence of this law, because evil and falsehood are so multiform and self-contradictory that universal agreement is obtainable only with respect to what is true and good.[60]

Such *"consensus gentium"* as evidence of what is prescribed by natural reason must be distinguished from the consent or agreement (in the sense of a binding contract, rather than a uniformity of opinion) which is the basis of the third type of law recognized by Grotius. This is called "secondary law of nations."

In the *Law of War and Peace* this category is called "law of nations" *simpliciter*, and is classified, along with civil law, as a species of "human volitional law" (*jus voluntarium humanum*).[61] It is made up of rules which nations are

[60] "Est quidem ista ratio nostro vitio obnubilata plurimum, non ita tamen, quin conspicua restent semina divinae lucis, quae in consensu gentium maxime apparent. Cum enim malum falsumque sit natura sui quodammodo infinitum atque insuper sibi repugnans, concordia universalis nisi ad bonum et verum esse non potest. Placuit autem plerisque hunc ipsum consensum jus naturae secundarium, seu jus gentium primarium appellare. . . ." *D.J.P.*, 12; *L.P.B.*, 12. "Jure primo gentium, quod et naturale interdum dicimus. . . ." *D.J.P.*, 215; *L.P.B.*, 227. See pp. 62–63, below. See also *D.J.P.*, 33; *L.P.B.*, 33.

[61] "Annectendum nunc illud est, esse quoddam jus mixtum ex jure gentium et civili, sive jus gentium quod recte ac proprie *secundarium* dicitur." *D.J.P.*, 26; *L.P.B.*, 26. See pp. 64, 74, below. Civil law is defined in *De Jure Praedae* as "quod non est jus per se, sed ex alio." *D.J.P.*, 23; *L.P.B.*, 23. It cannot modify the law of nature or of nations. *D.J.P.*, 34, *L.P.B.*, 34; *D.J.P.*, 232, *L.P.B.*, 246; *D.J.P.*, 236, *L.P.B.*, 249.

bound by compact to observe, such as the inviolability of ambassadors, sepulture, and the like. Occasionally the term is used in referring to what is really nothing more than a widespread custom, such as slavery, contracts, and inheritance; but as usages of this sort were introduced individually and not by common consent, they may be repealed or abolished if a nation so chooses, and are not really part of the consensually established law of nations.[62]

The primary law of nations (or law of nature, to use the preferable terminology of the book of 1625) is based on reason and is unchanging and immutable,[63] as is the primary law of nature (or *jus divinum voluntarium*).[64] Both

[62] "Exempla dari possunt de legatis non violandis, quos omnes gentes quae republica utuntur aeque sanctos habent, de mortuis sepeliendis et alia ejusmodi. Sunt autem haec duorum generum. Alia enim pacti vim habent inter respublicas, ut quae modo diximus: alia non habent, quae receptae potius consuetudinis nomine, quam juris appellaverim. Sed tamen et haec juris gentium frequenter dicuntur, ut quae de servitute, de certis contractuum generibus et successionum ordine populi omnes aut plerique, cum seorsim singulis ita expediret, in eamdem formam imitatione aut fortuito statuerunt. Quare ab his institutis licet singulis recedere, quia nec communiter sed sigillatim introducta sunt." *D.J.P.*, 26–27; *L.P.B.*, 26–27. See p. 49, below. See also *D.J.P.*, 275–76; *L.P.B.*, 291.

[63] "Primum ergo illud positum sit jure gentium primario jubente, cujus ratio perpetua est et immutabilis, licere Batavis quibusvis cum gentibus negotiari." *D.J.P.*, 205; *L.P.B.*, 218. "Commercandi igitur libertas ex jure est primario gentium, quod naturalem et perpetuam causam habet, ideoque tolli non potest, et si posset, non tamen posset nisi omnium gentium consensu: tantum abest ut ullo modo gens aliqua gentes duas inter se contrahere volentes juste impediat." *D.J.P.*, 244–45, *L.P.B.*, 257. See also *D.J.P.*, 301; *L.P.B.*, 319.

[64] "Jus enim naturae, cum a divina veniat providentia esse immutabile. Hujus autem juris naturalis partem esse jus gentium primaevum, quod dicitur, diversum a jure gentium secundario sive positivo: quorum posterius mutari potest, prius non potest. Nam si qui mores cum jure gentium primaevo repugnent, hi non humani sunt,

species of law, Grotius argued, gave the Dutch the right to trade with the Indies and the right to make war on the Portuguese for interfering with that right.

All law is divided, according to Grotius, into divine and human.[65] Divine law includes the law of nature and of nations.[66] Moreover, what is prescribed by the law of nature (for example, the law of war) is necessarily part of the law of nations.[67] As an example of the distinction drawn by Grotius between the two types of *jus gentium* may be cited his discussion of the question whether ownership, as well as possession, of enemy property passes by capture. An affirmative answer is given, based upon the "positive," not the "natural" law of nations. The law of prize is rooted in both types of *jus gentium*, as well as in the law of nature.[68]

It is thus evident that the legal philosophy which under-

---

ipso judice, set ferini, corruptelae et abusus, non leges et usus." *D.J.P.*, 237; *L.P.B.*, 250. See also *D.J.P.*, 33; *L.P.B.*, 33.

[65] *D.J.P.*, 40; *L.P.B.*, 40.

[66] *D.J.P.*, 34; *L.P.B.*, 34. The law of nature was flourishing in its purest state in the time of Abraham; says Grotius: "temporibus, quibus jus naturae purissimum vigebat." *D.J.P.*, 138; *L.P.B.*, 141.

[67] "Est autem bellum ejus generis, quia quod jus est naturae idem est jus gentium necessario, accedente scilicet ratione. . . ." *D.J.P.*, 33; *L.P.B.*, 33. "Juris gentium jus belli pars est. . . ." *D.J.P.*, 51; *L.P.B.*, 50. "Quod enim belli, id est gentium jure. . . ." *D.J.P.*, 333; *L.P.B.*, 356.

[68] "Omnino ausim affirmare jure gentium primario, quod ex natura defluit, hoc ipsum non contingere. . . . Sed defendi potest jure gentium secundario, quod esse sui origine civile diximus, idem illud procedere." *D.J.P.*, 119; *L.J.B.*, 120–21. "Jure igitur gentium, non illo naturali, sed positivo et quasi de pacto saltem inter plerosque populos inito, *justa rerum . . . captarum acquisitio . . . datur*. . . ." *D.J.P.*, 122; *L.P.B.*, 124. See pp. 42, 47, 49, below, and *D.J.P.*, 280; *L.P.B.*, 296; *D.J.P.*, 50; *L.P.B.*, 49, 50.

lies *De Jure Praedae* is essentially the same as that which appears in *De Jure Belli ac Pacis*. The only difference is that in the later work Grotius cleared away the confusing terminology of "primary" and "secondary" types of law, which he inherited from previous writers, and adopted a more meaningful nomenclature and one more closely in accord with his own ideas.[69]

The youthful Grotius, perhaps less self-confident than he was twenty years later, and in any event writing to persuade public opinion rather than to instruct statesmen, may have felt in his earlier treatise that he must eschew innovations and construct an impressive apparatus of erudition, such as is displayed in his complex scheme of nine rules and thirteen laws. As a more mature jurist, in the polished cosmopolitan world of Paris in 1625, he enjoyed a greater freedom to clarify his systematic concepts.

IV.

Turning now to the discussions regarding the lawfulness of war and prize contained in Chapters II–X of *De Jure Praedae*, we note that the theme and treatment closely parallel the line of thought familiar to readers of the *Law of War and Peace*. Indeed, it is sometimes said that *De Jure Praedae* is the first edition of the masterpiece of 1625.[70]

Grotius begins by inquiring in Chapter III whether war

[69] Note the third and fourth sentences of the passage quoted in note 62 above. See *L.P.B.*, xxi. The natural law of Grotius is positive. Willem J. M. Van Eysinga, "De beteekenis van de Groot voor het internationale recht," *De Gids*, Vol. CVIII, No. 11 (Nov., 1945), 76, 79, 86; van Eysinga, *Gids voor de Groots De Iure Belli ac Pacis*, 3–4.

[70] *Schets*, 24.

can ever be just.[71] An affirmative answer is given by the evidence of God's will found in nature and scripture.[72] As the law of war is part of the universal law of nature, in force *semper et ubique*, it follows that war is permitted even after Christ and among Christians.[73]

In Chapter IV Grotius considers whether the capture of prize is ever just. He concludes that since war is just if it is a means of enforcing legal rights,[74] so prize is by the same token justified: "in prize we obtain our right by war."[75] As killing in war is not murder, so the capture of enemy property is not robbery.[76] Prize is permitted by the law of nature and the law of nations.[77] By analogy to judicial procedure where execution extends not only to the amount of the original claim but also includes the costs of suit, Grotius points out that the party waging just war may capture enemy property to reimburse the costs of war.[78] Prize, like victory, is from God.[79] It is permitted by all law to Christians and against Christians.[80]

[71] *D.J.P.*, 31; *L.P.B.*, 31.   [72] *D.J.P.*, 35; *L.P.B.*, 35.

[73] "Si ergo jus est semper, etiam post Christum: si ubique, etiam inter Christianos." *D.J.P.*, 33; *L.P.B..*, 33. "Bellare igitur licet." *D.J.P.*, 36; *L.P.B.*, 36. See also *D.J.P.*, 38; *L.P.B.*, 38; *D.J.P.*, 42; *L.P.B.*, 42.

[74] Equivalent to judicial procedure, as we have seen in the text at note 39 above.

[75] "Et in praeda jus nostrum per bellum adipiscimur. . . ." *D.J.P.*, 43; *L.P.B.*, 43.

[76] *D.J.P.*, 45; *L.P.B.*, 45. See also *D.J.P.*, 52; *L.P.B.*, 51.

[77] *D.J.P.*, 50; *L.P.B.*, 49.

[78] *D.J.P.*, 47–48; *L.P.B.*, 47. See also *D.J.P.*, 134, *L.P.B.*, 137; *D.J.P.*, 254, *L.P.B.*, 267.

[79] "Sicut igitur victoria sic etiam praeda a Deo. . . ." *D.J.P.*, 52; *L.P.B.*, 52. See Jefferson's motto, "Ab eo libertas a quo spiritus." Dumbauld, *The Declaration of Independence and What It Means Today*, 58–59.

[80] *D.J.P.*, 57; *L.P.B.*, 57.

Very briefly in Chapter V Grotius asserts that all prize is lawful that is taken in a just war, and that all war is just which is waged only for lawful causes.[81] It is therefore necessary to determine: (*a*) who may wage a just war; (*b*) for what causes, and against whom; (*c*) in what manner and to what extent; and (*d*) for what purpose.[82]

Chapter VI demonstrates that a private war (*bellum privatum*) may be justly waged with the help of allies and subjects (*subditi*, such as sons, servants, and the like),[83] and that a public war (*bellum publicum*) may be justly waged by a state or government with the help of its subjects and allies.[84]

The causes of a just war are discussed in Chapter VII. This chapter and the two that follow it, as well as Chapter III, were especially important as sources for the *Law of War and Peace*.[85] Grotius declares that war being the execution of a right,[86] the cause of a just war is necessarily a legal right.[87]

Referring to the first, second, fifth, and sixth of the thirteen laws set forth in Chapter II, Grotius classifies the legal rights which justify war into these causes: (*a*) self-defense; (*b*) protection of property, including intangible rights and good name;[88] (*c*) enforcement of an obligation due, as

[81] D.J.P., 58; L.P.B., 58–59.
[82] D.J.P., 59; L.P.B., 59.
[83] D.J.P., 62; L.P.B., 62.
[84] D.J.P., 66; L.P.B., 65.
[85] See p. 66, below.
[86] See notes 39, 42, and 44, above.
[87] "Cum igitur bellum justum juris sit exsecutio, id de quo justo bello certatur, jus sit necesse est." D.J.P., 66; L.P.B., 66.
[88] See Iago's speech in Shakespeare's *Othello*, Act III, scene 3, line 155. Regarding Portuguese slander against the Dutch, see D.J.P., 176–77; L.P.B., 183–84; D.J.P., 196, L.P.B., 206.

a debt under a contract, and the like; and (*d*) punishment of wrongs and injuries.[89]

Hence Grotius concludes that, for those acting on their own account, it is a just cause of war to defend life or property, to recover what has been taken or is owing, or to punish wrong.[90] They may treat as enemies not only states or individuals who commit an injury directly, but also states which protect citizens who have done so, and the allies and subjects of the wrongdoers.[91]

In the case of those who are not acting on their own account, but are subject to the authority of another, a war has a just cause if it is ordered by a superior, unless the subject finds that it conflicts with his own conscience to a degree amounting to probability.[92] Mere doubt is not sufficient reason for disobedience to authority, but in a clear case it is the duty of a subject to heed his own conscience.[93] Hence, in the case of subjects it is possible for a war to be just on both sides,[94] though this is impossible in the case of those acting on their own account.[95]

[89] D.J.P., 67–68; L.P.B., 67. In *Law of War and Peace* Grotius varies this analysis slightly, and also develops the whole repertory of substantive rights, violations of which may cause war. See p. 66, below. See also D.J.P., 69; L.P.B., 69. To wage unjust war is a crime meriting severe punishment. D.J.P., 255; L.P.B., 268.

[90] D.J.P., 71; L.P.B., 70.   [91] D.J.P., 75; L.P.B., 75

[92] "Subditis id bellum justam habet causam, quod jubetur a superiore, dum ratio probabilis subditorum non repugnet." D.J.P., 80; L.P.B., 80. "Justum est bellum subditis in eos, quos superiores bello peti jubent, ratione probabili subditorum non repugnante." D.J.P., 82; L.P.B., 82.

[93] D.J.P., 78; L.P.B., 78: "Nec obstat, quod dubitas ne feceris. . . . in dubio obediendum. . . ."

[94] "Subditorum respectu bellum ex utraque parte justum datur, praecedente scilicet jussu, cui ratio probabilis non repugnet." D.J.P., 84; L.P.B., 84.

[95] D.J.P., 83; L.P.B., 83. See p. 61, below.

44

Chapter VIII deals with the form and manner of making war. Grotius first answers the objection that private war can never be justified because the ninth and twelfth laws (set forth in Chapter II) forbid self-help without prior resort to judicial procedure. His answer is that such procedure may be temporarily or permanently unavailable. The latter is true of deserts, islands, and places where no civil society has been established. In such a case, by natural law, everyone is authorized to execute his own right.[96] This power includes punishment of wrongdoing.[97] Grotius concludes that private war is justly waged to the extent that judicial procedure is unavailable.[98]

A formal declaration of war is unnecessary, according to Grotius, if a demand for justice has been made without avail or if the other party first commences hostilities.[99]

Grotius next passes to the consideration of what is re-

[96] *D.J.P.*, 88; *L.P.B.*, 88: ". . . juris quisque sui exsecutor." See also *D.J.P.*, 29; *L.P.B.*, 29; *D.J.P.*, 94, *L.P.B.*, 94; *D.J.P.*, 130; *L.P.B.*, 133; *D.J.P.*, 133, *L.P.B.*, 136; *D.J.P.*, 260, *L.P.B.*, 274. Natural liberty existed before civil society was organized. "[Libertas] a natura sit, imperium a facto hominis." *D.J.P.*, 285; *L.P.B.*, 301. "Deus enim qui cuncta creavit in sua perfectione, non rempublicam creavit sed homines duos. Itaque tantum societas humana erat, civitas non erat." *D.J.P.*, 92; *L.P.B.*, 92.

[97] Private war is thus justified under the fourth of the causes of war specified above as well as under the first three. *D.J.P.*, 89, 91, 94; *L.P.B.*, 89, 92, 94. See p. 60, below. "Lex igitur illa quae maleficos punire jubet, cum ex jure naturae sive gentium descendat, civili societate et lege est antiquior." *D.J.P.*, 90; *L.P.B.*, 90.

[98] "Eatenus juste bellum privatum suscipitur, quatenus judicium deficit." *D.J.P.*, 95; *L.P.B.*, 95. "Quatenus enim ista [judicia] deficiunt eatenus vis, hoc est privata secundum naturam exsecutio, justa est." *D.J.P.*, 86; *L.P.B.*, 87. See p. 66, below.

[99] *D.J.P.*, 95; *L.P.B.*, 96; *D.J.P.*, 100–101, *L.P.B.*, 101–102; *D.J.P.*, 276, *L.P.B.*, 292. A reversion to the law of nature then occurs. See p. 69, below.

quired and permitted in regard to the manner of waging war.[100]

The state is responsible for the wrongs done by its citizens if it does not do justice.[101] Conversely citizens are responsible for the actions of the state.[102] Hence belligerent action may rightfully extend as far as the right being enforced and the persons bound thereby.[103] Accordingly the property of subjects may be captured and applied to the captor's use, "for nothing is more just than to seek by arms what can not be had otherwise."[104] Subjects who by hostile acts, or even innocently, interfere with the enforcement of right may be killed or injured.[105] But subjects who do not impede belligerent operations may not be slain or harmed in body, though their property may be taken.[106] However, the property of strangers, not belonging to the enemy, is not subject to capture[107] unless it is contraband useful in war.[108]

Grotius declares that the law of nations requires faith to be kept, even with a perfidious enemy.[109] This emphasis on good faith is also found in the *Law of War and Peace* as

[100] "Videndum . . . quid . . . in bello gerendo desideretur et quantum illis permittatur. . . ." D.J.P., 101; L.P.B., 103. This is the topic of Book III of *De Jure Belli ac Pacis*. See p. 68, below.

[101] D.J.P., 104–105, L.P.B., 106; D.J.P., 259, L.P.B., 273; D.J.P., 261, L.P.B., 276.

[102] D.J.P., 106, L.P.B., 107; D.J.P., 259, L.P.B., 273.

[103] ". . . eatenus bellum . . . juste geritur, quatenus intra id jus manet, quo de agitur, intraque personas ei juri obligatas." D.J.P., 107, L.P.B., 108; D.J.P., 260–61, L.P.B., 275.

[104] ". . . nihil est justius quam armis repeti quod aliter non potest. . . ." D.J.P., 111; L.P.B., 112.

[105] D.J.P., 109–10; L.P.B., 111–12.

[106] D.J.P., 111; L.P.B., 113. See also D.J.P., 115; L.P.B., 116.

[107] D.J.P., 113; L.P.B., 114.

[108] D.J.P., 114; L.P.B., 115.

[109] D.J.P., 115; L.P.B., 117.

well as in the earliest known writing of Grotius on the law of nations, composed in 1601 or 1602 but never published by him.[110]

With respect to subjects not acting for their own account, Grotius holds that they may wage war[111] to such extent as their superiors may order.[112] Likewise they may lawfully take possession of enemy property on either side if an order has been given which there is no probable ground for considering unjust insofar as their own consciences are concerned.[113]

May subjects also acquire full ownership of such captured property? Here Grotius draws a distinction between the primary law of nations (or law of nature) which he believes does not permit such a transfer of property without the owner's consent, and the secondary law of nations (of civil origin) which allows it. The practice came into vogue because experience proved that citizens would fight more bravely if they knew there was no hope of recovering their property after it was captured by the enemy.[114]

Grotius concludes this chapter with a few comments on *postliminium*,[115] and with the explanation that the rules of war he has described apply only to conflicts between "legitimate enemies"[116] and not in the case of piracy or civil war.

[110] See pp. 71–72, below.
[111] They may not undertake war: "Nunc quomodo subditi juste bellum gerant, explicandum est: neque enim ab illis suscipi satis patet." *D.J.P.*, 117; *L.P.B.*, 118.
[112] *D.J.P.*, 118; *L.P.B.*, 119.   [113] *D.J.P.*, 119; *L.P.B.*, 120.
[114] *D.J.P.*, 119; *L.P.B.*, 121. See also *D.J.P.*, 122; *L.P.B.*, 124.
[115] See p. 70, below.
[116] "Inter legitimos igitur hostes jura ista obtinent. . . ." *D.J.P.*, 121; *L.P.B.*, 123. A legitimate enemy is one that follows the probable authority of a government. See *Framework*, 89.

The purpose of war is discussed briefly in Chapter IX. Affirming, with William Penn, that "peace is the fruit of justice," Grotius asserts that the purpose of war is the establishment of a just and honorable peace.[117] Such a peace is nothing other than the warding off of wrong or, what comes to the same thing, the establishment of right.[118] The right vindicated need not be the belligerent's own but may be that of another, for example, that of an ally. It is often advantageous to the security of all that injuries to individual parties be prevented.[119]

Hence those who have themselves suffered injury and seek to capture enemy property do so with righteous purpose, namely to obtain what is due them, which is the prize captured.[120] Those who are subject to the authority of another, and do not wage war on their own account, wage it with righteous purpose when they do so in obedience to their superior.[121]

The theme of Chapter X is: "Who becomes the owner of property captured as prize?"[122] Grotius takes the position that since war is equivalent to judicial enforcement of a legal right, no one but the possessor of the right is entitled to the prize.[123] In the case of a private war, this is the "prin-

[117] D.J.P., 123; L.P.B., 125.

[118] "Pax igitur bellanti proposita nihil est aliud quam injuriae depulsio, sive quod in idem recidit juris adeptio, non utique sui, sed interdum etiam alieni. . . ." D.J.P., 124; L.P.B., 126.

[119] ". . . interest enim securitatis omnium arceri injurias. . . ." D.J.P., 125; L.P.B., 127. See D.J.P., 40, 49, 90, 251, 255; L.P.B., 40, 49, 90, 264, 268.

[120] "Hi vero qui damnum passi sunt ipsi, hoc dum reparant, etiam propter praedam recte militant, hoc est propter juris sui consecutionem, qua in praeda consistit." D.J.P., 126; L.P.B., 129.

[121] D.J.P., 127; L.P.B., 129.   [122] D.J.P., 128; see L.P.B., 130.

[123] "Nemo igitur recte dominus fiet praedae, nisi qui jus, hoc est causam crediti habet." D.J.P., 128; L.P.B., 130.

48

cipal author of the war,"[124] unless a different arrangement is agreed upon.[125] In the case of a public war, the state is obviously the party whose right is being enforced and is also the party bearing the cost of the war. Hence the prize belongs to the state, not to the individual captors;[126] but here, too, the state may assign it by general law or by a special dispensation to others, usually the soldiers or sailors participating in the capture.[127]

These conclusions are buttressed by extensive comments on Roman history and Roman law in which Grotius undertakes to refute writers who claimed that prize belonged to the captors rather than to the state. One argument used by Grotius is that by the primary law of nations (law of nature) there was no distinction between movable and immovable property, and that it was undisputed that land won from the enemy became public property.[128] In another passage he argues that the rule of Roman law assigning movable property to the captors was one of positive law rather than of the law of nations.[129]

[124] ". . . dico rerum bello privato captarum dominum fieri eum, qui belli auctor sit principalis, quoad jus suum consecutus sit. . . ." *D.J.P.*, 134; see *L.P.B.*, 137. See also *D.J.P.*, 138; *L.P.B.*, 141.

[125] *D.J.P.*, 138; *L.P.B.*, 142.

[126] *D.J.P.*, 139; *L.P.B.*, 142. ". . . praedam naturaliter esse publicam ante distributionem." *D.J.P.*, 140; *L.P.B.*, 143. See pp. 69–70, below.

[127] *D.J.P.*, 151–52; *L.P.B.*, 156. See also *D.J.P.*, 162; *L.P.B.*, 167.

[128] "Illud enim jus gentium, quod naturae dici potest, nullam habet causam in acquisitionibus distinguendi inter res mobiles et immobiles: . . . Agros autem ex hostibus captos sicut et civitates publicas fieri et non occupantium singulorum, omni historia . . . evidens est. . . ." *D.J.P.*, 141; *L.P.B.*, 145.

[129] "Id enim non ex primario ut diximus gentium jure procedit,

In this chapter occurs the quotation from Livy[130] which may have suggested to Grotius the title of his masterpiece of 1625[131] as well as another passage which emphasizes the theme, so basic to *De Jure Belli ac Pacis*, that war does not do away with law between enemies.[132] The primary rule of the law of war is also proclaimed to be that everything is lawful which is necessary in order to enforce a right.[133]

V.

Following his *dogmatica*, as has been noted, Grotius in Chapter XI sets forth the *historica*, in which he recounts the history of Dutch trade with the Indies and of Portuguese attempts to suppress it. It is not necessary to summarize this historical portion of the treatise in detail. The fundamental point is that the events narrated proved the existence of a state of war between the Portuguese and the Dutch, and consequently the lawfulness of the capture of the *Catharina*.

Grotius argues that when Philip II became King of Portugal at a time when he was engaged in war with the

sed ex jure positivo, cujus pars magna sunt consuetudines. Deinde non ex condicto venit, ut respublicas obliget, sed quasi fortuito consensu, a quo singulis populis, ubi ita videtur, recedere liberum est. . . ." *D.J.P.*, 157; *L.P.B.*, 162. See note 62, above.

[130] "[S]unt et belli sicut et pacis jura. . . ." (Livy, Bk. 5, c. 27.) *D.J.P.*, 129; *L.P.B.*, 131.

[131] See note 13, above.

[132] "Tollit bellum communionem civilem, non illam humani generis." *D.J.P.*, 129; *L.P.B.*, 132. See p. 73, below.

[133] ". . . in bello id omne licere, quod ad juris exsecutionem necessarium est. . . ." *D.J.P.*, 130; *L.P.B.*, 132–33. See p. 69, below, and *Framework*, 91.

Depositum cæli, quod iure Batavia mater
Horret, et vaud credit se peperisse sibi
Talem oculis, talem ore tulit te maxime Hugo.
Instar crede somnis, cætera crede Dei.

D. Heinsius A° 1614.

HUGO GROTIUS

After a portrait by Mierevelt

THE PRISON CHAMBER OF GROTIUS AT LOEVESTEIN CASTLE

Dutch (which led to his being deposed as ruler of the Netherlands[134] and to the independence of the Dutch under the Union of Utrecht), the Dutch and Portuguese became enemies,[135] although trade between them continued. This contention was upheld by the prize court when it condemned the *Catharina*.[136]

In colorful language expressing his passionate, patriotic sentiments, Grotius describes the brutal slaying and mistreatment of the Dutch by the Portuguese on numerous occasions.[137] The Dutch in spite of the existence of a state of war had never resorted to hostilities.[138]

In Chapter XII, published separately as *Mare Liberum,* Grotius demonstrates that the war of the Dutch against the Portuguese was just under the principles of international law set forth in his *dogmatica,* and that the *Catharina* was good prize.[139] In this chapter the discussion proceeds upon the assumption that the East India Company was engaging in a private war.

Laying aside the long-standing conflict between the Dutch and Portuguese, and considering the case of the East India Company as if it were composed of French, German, or English citizens, Grotius bases his argument upon the right to free trade and freedom of the seas given by the law of nature.[140]

[134] See p. 18, above.
[135] *D.J.P.,* 168; *L.P.B.,* 174.
[136] Willem J. M. van Eysinga, "Grotius et la Chine," *Grotiana,* Vol. VII (1939), 20, 23. At 28–33 is given the text of the court's judgment; for which see also *D.J.P.,* 350–54; *L.P.B.,* 375–79.
[137] See note 21, above.
[138] *D.J.P.,* 203; *L.P.B.,* 214.
[139] *D.J.P.,* 262, *L.P.B.,* 276; *D.J.P.,* 266, *L.P.B.,* 281.
[140] *D.J.P.,* 204–205; *L.P.B.,* 217–18.

He proves that the sea cannot be monopolized by virtue of discovery, occupation, papal grant, prescription, or custom.[141] Likewise the right to trade with one nation cannot be monopolized by another nation.[142] Interference by the Portuguese with the exercise of these rights of navigation and commerce constituted just cause for war.[143]

Chapter XIII shows that the East India Company was justified in capturing the *Catharina*, on the assumption that the Dutch seamen were engaged, not in a private war, but in a public war declared by authority of the States of Holland.[144] As subjects it was their duty to treat as enemies those so designated by their government.[145] The *Catharina* fell within the express provisions of edicts directed against subjects of the King of Spain, and against ships coming from colonies of Portugal or going to a Portuguese port.[146] Finally, the prize is sustained on an additional independent ground, namely, that the Company was engaged as an ally in public war on behalf of the native Indian states.[147]

In Chapter XIV Grotius avers, having completed his inquiry as to lawfulness, that capture of this prize was honorable because it was based upon the immutable law of nature.[148] Moreover, it is noble to battle against enemies

[141] D.J.P., 207, 223, 231-33, 234, 237; L.P.B., 220, 236, 244, 247-48, 250. Grotius rejects the view that Christendom constitutes a single state. D.J.P., 51, L.P.B., 51; D.J.P., 210, L.P.B., 222.

[142] D.J.P., 245; L.P.B., 257-58.

[143] D.J.P., 250; L.P.B., 263; D.J.P., 293; L.P.B., 310.

[144] D.J.P., 268, L.P.B., 283; D.J.P., 299, L.P.B., 316-17. Grotius patriotically shows that the States of Holland had sovereign power to declare war, since all authority comes from the people. D.J.P., 270-72; L.P.B., 285-87.

[145] D.J.P., 286, L.P.B., 302; D.J.P., 295, L.P.B., 312.

[146] D.J.P., 288; L.P.B., 305.

[147] D.J.P., 297-98; L.P.B., 314-15.

[148] D.J.P., 301; L.P.B., 319.

who wrong one's native land.[149] "We see justice in undertaking war, bravery in waging it, and fairness in concluding it."[150] Furthermore, prize brings no gain, but merely reimburses for losses, and nothing can be more honorable than that.[151] Grotius speaks with stirring language in this chapter and declares that they hardly deserve to be called men, much less Dutchmen, who would suffer their countrymen to lose their lives but hesitate to strip their enemies of property.[152]

The same passionate strain pervades Chapter XV, the final chapter, in which Grotius urges that prize is expedient. He shows that individual wealth benefits the public and that revenue from prizes supports the public treasury[153] at the expense of enemies rather than of taxpayers.[154] Grotius praises commerce[155] and the Dutch seafarers.[156] He stresses the double importance of gaining the Indian trade and keeping it from the enemy.[157] It would be folly to refuse the benefits bestowed by the law of nations and the approval of the government.[158]

In conclusion Grotius exhorts the merchants to manifest Dutch faith among the most distant peoples and to defend the holy right of commerce against all injuries. He then

149 *D.J.P.*, 302; *L.P.B.*, 320.
150 "Videmus in suscipiendo bello justitiam, in gerendo fortitudinem, in deponendo aequitatem." *D.J.P.*, 310; see *L.P.B.*, 329.
151 *D.J.P.*, 312; *L.P.B.*, 332.
152 *D.J.P.*, 315; *L.P.B.*, 335; *D.J.P.*, 333; *L.P.B.*, 357.
153 *D.J.P.*, 318; *L.P.B*, 339.
154 *D.J.P.*, 318; *L.P.B.*, 340.
155 *D.J.P.*, 321; *L.P.B.*, 343.
156 *D.J.P.*, 329–32; *L.P.B.*, 352–55.
157 *D.J.P.*, 327; *L.P.B.*, 349.
158 *D.J.P.*, 333; *L.P.B.*, 356.

addresses God in the previously quoted prayer for the welfare of Holland and the destruction of her enemies.[159]

CONCLUSION

From the foregoing analysis of *De Jure Praedae* it is apparent how extensively that treatise, written when Grotius was a young lawyer, contributed to the formation of the doctrines developed in his better-known work, *De Jure Belli ac Pacis*. Substantially identical in both treatises are: (*a*) the basic philosophical groundwork of natural law speculation; (*b*) the fundamental theme of just war as a legal remedy akin to judicial procedure and available for the punishment of international wrongdoing; and (*c*) the code of binding rules relating to the manner in which warfare must be conducted.

Present in the earlier work, but absent in the later, are: (*a*) a scholastic formalism, evinced in the nine rules and thirteen laws of Chapter II; (*b*) the *historica* or narrative of events which formed the background of the specific litigation involving the *Catharina*;[160] (*c*) the legal argumentation which related to the circumstances of that particular case; (*d*) the discussion as to the honorableness and expediency of prize; and (*e*) the patriotic fervor and zest with which Grotius sought to persuade his fellow countrymen and inflame their zeal.[161]

---

[159] D.J.P., 351; L.P.B., 365–66. See text at note 19, above.

[160] Grotius may have planned to use this material in historical writings. D.J.P., x.

[161] Regarding this purpose Grotius later wrote: ". . . operam dedi ut ad tuenda fortiter, quae tam feliciter coepissent, nostrorum animos inflammarem. . . ." D.J.P., ix. According to van Eysinga, *Schets*, 27, an even stronger expression of patriotic sentiment is found in an earlier work of Grotius, *Parallelon Rerumpublicarum*, as to which see

In other words, in his later treatment of the law of war in general[162] Grotius merely eliminated the specific facts and arguments which had pertinence only in connection with the particular case which was the occasion for writing *De Jure Praedae*. He retained and expanded the material which related to the underlying legal principles involved. At the same time he abandoned didactic artificiality and partisan advocacy in favor of a more mature and disinterested scholarship.

The principal feature present in the later work, but absent in the earlier, is the elaboration of the system of substantive legal rights, violation of which furnishes a just cause for war.[163] This treatment of the "law of peace" justifies the twofold development implicit in the title of the book. There is also noticeable in *De Jure Belli ac Pacis* a desire on the part of Grotius to mitigate the ferocity of warfare, and he introduces qualifications which weaken the broad sweep of belligerent rights.[164] The style is smoother,

p. 72, below. As to his intentions regarding *De Jure Belli ac Pacis*, see *Framework*, 28, and pp. 75–76, below.

[162] *De Jure Belli ac Pacis* may have been begun as a work on the law of war alone. In several passages it speaks of being a treatise "de jure belli." *Framework*, 156–57. Hamaker's conclusion that the material on the law of peace was added later (*D.J.P.*, x) van Vollenhoven states is purely a supposition.

[163] See pp. 66–67, below. Meanwhile Grotius had written his celebrated textbook on Dutch civil law. See also *Framework*, 63, 103. There are numerous references, however, in *De Jure Praedae* to the "societas humani generis" which the law of peace governs (*Framework*, 1, 11; van Eysinga, *Gids voor de Groots De Iure Belli ac Pacis*, 3, 11), *D.J.P.*, 19; *L.P.B.*, 19; *D.J.P.*, 21, *L.P.B.*, 21; *D.J.P.*, 60, *L.P.B.*, 61; *D.J.P.*, 90, *L.P.B.*, 90; *D.J.P.*, 92, *L.P.B.*, 92; *D.J.P.*, 137, *L.P.B.*, 140; *D.J.P.*, 206, *L.P.B.*, 218; *D.J.P.*, 218, *L.P.B.*, 231; *D.J.P.*, 249, *L.P.B.*, 261; *D.J.P.*, 249, *L.P.B.*, 262; *D.J.P.*, 256, *L.P.B.*, 270; *D.J.P.*, 297, *L.P.B.*, 314; *D.J.P.*, 311, *L.P.B.*, 331.

[164] See p. 31, above, and p. 70, below.

but less spirited. Mars yields to Minerva. The "marvel of Holland" had become "the jurisconsult of humanity."[165]

[165] The French king Henri IV, greeting the fifteen-year-old Grotius in 1598, exclaimed: "Voilà le miracle de Hollande." *Schets*, 10. The Italian jurist Vico called Grotius "generis humani jurisconsultus." *Opera*, III, 42, quoted in van Eysinga, "De Beteekenis van de Groot voor het Internationale Recht," *De Gids*, Vol. CVIII, No. 11 (Nov., 1945), 76.

On the Law of War and Peace
De Jure Belli ac Pacis

HVGONIS GROTII

DE IVRE BELLI

AC PACIS

LIBRI TRES.

In quibus ius naturae & Gentium: item iuris
publici praecipua explicantur.

PARISIIS,
Apud NICOLAVM BVON, in via Iacobea, sub signis
S. Claudij, & Hominis Siluestris.

M.DC.XXV.
CVM PRIVILEGIO REGIS.

With the above title page[1] there appeared in Paris, in
1625, the first edition[2] of the memorable treatise on the

[1] From the Library of Congress copy.

[2] Jesse Reeves, "The First Edition of Grotius' De Jure Belli ac
Pacis, 1625," *American Journal of International Law*, Vol. XIX,
No. 1 (Jan., 1925), 12; Philip C. Molhuysen, "Over de editio princeps
van Grotius' De Iure Belli ac Pacis," in *Mededeelingen der Konink-*

law of war and peace by Hugo Grotius which earned for him the designation "father of international law."[3]

Other editions with corrections prepared by the author were published at Amsterdam by Blaeu in 1631, 1632, 1642, and 1646.[4] In 1929 a total of seventy-eight editions and translations had appeared.[5]

---

lijke Akademie Van Wetenschappen, Afdeeling Letterkunde, Vol. LX, Series B., No. 1 (1925). Grotius began to gather material for his *opus magnum* as early as November, 1622. Much of the writing was done in pleasant rural surroundings at Balagny, though there are some signs of haste in composition. *Writings,* I, 353, 520; *Framework,* 29.

[3] Grotius is rightfully accorded this title because of the influence of his book although many of his ideas can be found in the writings of his precursors. Roscoe Pound, "Grotius in the Science of Law," *American Journal of International Law,* Vol. XIX, No. 4 (Oct., 1925), 685; Willem J. M. van Eysinga, "Grotius (1625-1925)," *Revue de Droit International et de Legislation Comparée,* Vol. LII, No. 3 (1925), 269, 278; Carl von Kaltenborn, *Die Vorläufer des Hugo Grotius auf dem Gebiete des Ius naturae et gentium Sowie der Politik im Reformationszeitalter,* 22: "Grotius . . . alle seine Vorgänger überflügelte."

[4] *Writings,* I, 483. The best single source of material on Grotius is the series of articles in English, Dutch, and French reprinted in this volume (pp. 221–86, 349–602) of the collected writings of the late Professor Cornelis van Vollenhoven of Leyden. Death prevented preparation of the biography of Grotius which he had planned. His colleague, Judge W. J. M. van Eysinga, published a valuable sketch on the tercentenary of the death of Grotius: *Huigh de Groot, Een Schets.*

[5] *Writings,* I, 563. The first translation was into Dutch the year after the work appeared. The next was into English in 1654. French, German, and Italian versions appeared in 1687, 1707, and 1777, respectively. Jesse Reeves, "Grotius, De Jure Belli ac Pacis: A Bibliographical Account," *American Journal of International Law,* Vol. XIX, No. 2 (Apr., 1925), 251, 258. The fifth German translation and the first one in Japanese appeared in 1950. Kunz, Book Review, *American Journal of International Law,* Vol. XLV (1951), 610. For a bibliography of Grotius see H. C. Rogge, *Bibliotheca Grotiana;* and

Grotius did not intend, according to Professor van Vollenhoven, to write a textbook on international law in the modern[6] sense.[7] His theme was rather the law common to all mankind, the law of the universal human society which prevails on earth (*communis societas generis humani*).[8] He recognized that just as no national state can exist without law, so also the broader international society cannot exist without law.[9]

Thus the two principal topics treated by Grotius in his famous treatise are the legal obligations of human societies (including those that have sovereign power), and the procedure for enforcing such duties and punishing violations of law.[10] War was regarded by Grotius as a type of law-en-

ter Meulen and Diermanse, *Bibliographie des écrits imprimés de Hugo Grotius* [hereinafter cited as *Bibliographie*]. The twentieth century also saw versions in Russian (1915 and 1948), Spanish (1925), and Chinese (1937). In *Bibliographie* 112 items relate to editions and translations of *De Jure Belli ac Pacis*.

[6] By "modern" international law is meant the conventional system in vogue before the world wars which deals only with the mutual relations of states *inter sese* and rejects the notion that individuals have any rights or duties under international law. A still more "modern" trend, representing a recurrence to Grotius and the idea popularized in the Declaration of Independence that individuals possess legal rights not derived from the state, is gradually gaining acceptance today, particularly as regards war crimes and the humanitarian treatment of refugees and displaced persons without nationality. Dumbauld, *The Declaration of Independence and What It Means Today*, 58.

[7] *Writings*, I, 386, 390, 393; *Framework*, 1, 28; and his *De Jure Pacis*, 176.

[8] Grotius, *De Jure Belli ac Pacis* [hereinafter cited as *J.B.P.*], 2.20.44.4 (second book, twentieth chapter, forty-fourth section, fourth paragraph). Paragraph division was not introduced until the edition of 1667. *Writings*, I, 563. Likewise, in earlier editions the *Prolegomena* are not divided into numbered sections. See p. 55, above.

[9] *Framework*, 12; *Prolegomena* 23 in *J.B.P.*

[10] *Framework*, 66, 156; *J.B.P.*, 2.20.44.6.

forcement procedure akin to judicial remedies.[11] He did not, as van Vollenhoven strikingly observes, consider the "law of peace" and "law of war" as halves of something called international law as subsequent treatises have done; under the former topic he treated the "substantive law of duties binding on mankind," while under the latter he dealt with the remedial, procedural, or adjective law by which such duties were enforced.[12]

That states were subject to legal duties and to punishment for violations of law were vital features of the Grotian system.[13] According to van Vollenhoven, the teachings regarding punishment of states constitute the heart of the message of Grotius.[14] In keeping with this principle, those who were nonparticipants in a war were forbidden to hinder the party having a just cause or to aid the culprit.[15] Toward the end of the eighteenth century this rule was eclipsed by the vogue of Vattel,[16] who taught that both sides were to be treated as equally engaged in waging just

[11] Dumbauld, *Interim Measures of Protection in International Controversies*, 30; *Prolegomena* 25 in *J.B.P.*; J.B.P., 2.1.1.4, 2.1.2.1. See also p. 33, above.

[12] *Framework*, 101, 116. Regarding the substantive law or "law of peace," see pp. 66–67, below.

[13] *Framework*, 3, 13, 17, 31–34, 42; *Writings*, I, 393, 413, 461–68, 581–82.

[14] *Framework*, 80–87; *Writings*, I, 392–93, 411, 421–24, 461–68, 601–602; J.B.P., 2.20.40.1, 2.20.40.4, 2.20.44.1. Preceding writers (Victoria, Vasquez, Azorius, Molina, and Covarruvius) permitted punishment only by the party injured, or by a superior having civil jurisdiction over the culprit. Grotius held that the law of nature gave such power. J.B.P., 2.20.40.4: "Ponunt enim illi puniendi potestatem esse effectum proprium jurisdictionis civilis, cum nos eam sentiamus venire etiam ex jure naturali." See also p. 45, above.

[15] J.B.P., 2.17.3.1.

[16] Charles G. Fenwick, "The Authority of Vattel," *American Political Science Review*, Vol. VII, No. 3 (Aug., 1913), 395.

war. Thus the doctrine of neutrality took shape, and the principles of Grotius were neglected until they experienced a rebirth in the twentieth century, thanks to the efforts of Woodrow Wilson and the League of Nations.[17]

This picture of the significance of Grotius to the development of modern world government must not be permitted to obscure the fact (which van Vollenhoven himself recognized)[18] that Grotius in his passages dealing with "formal war" (*bellum sollenne*),[19] concedes that such a war may be regarded as just on both sides[20] and that other nations should not try to decide which party is right.[21] How does this differ from Vattel?

The law of mankind which Grotius expounded was considered as binding not only upon sovereign states as such in their mutual dealings,[22] but also upon persons not yet organized as a unit of political society, as well as upon individuals belonging to different nations or situated in uninhabited or uncivilized areas, and even upon pirates and outlaws.[23] Civil law within a single state was excluded by Grotius from the scope of his treatise, since civil rights are enforceable by judicial procedure, not by war.[24]

[17] *Writings*, I, 430–37; *Writings*, II, 418, 423, 438, 441.

[18] *Framework*, 153–55.

[19] Defined as a war carried on on both sides by the highest political authority, and declared in acccordance with due formality. *J.B.P.*, 1.3.4.1, 3.3.5.–.

[20] *J.B.P.*, 3.4.3.–.

[21] *J.B.P.*, 2.23.13.5, 3.4.4.–.

[22] *Prolegomena* 1 in *J.B.P.*: "jus illud, quod inter populos plures aut populorum rectores intercedit, sive ab ipsa natura profecta, aut divinis constitutum legibus, sive moribus et pacto tacito introductum."

[23] *J.B.P.*, 1.1.1.–, 2.20.40.4, 3.19.2.2, 2.13.15.2, 3.20.32.2, 2.20.17.2–3; *Framework*, 1, 3, 13, 17, 30, 42, 156.

[24] *J.B.P.*, 2.7.1.–. Civil law is defined as that which emanates from the supreme power in the state. The state is defined as a "perfect

Defining two of the three terms appearing in the title of his book,[25] Grotius states that by "war" he means "the status of those contending by force, as such."[26]

Law (*jus*) is analyzed as meaning "what is just," namely, what is not contrary to the nature of a society of rational creatures.[27] Law also signifies a rule (*lex*) of moral action obliging to what is right (as distinguished from what is merely honorable or expedient).[28]

Following Aristotle,[29] Grotius divides law into two classifications: natural law (*jus naturale*) and volitional law (*jus voluntarium*). Natural law is defined as the "dictate of right reason, indicating with respect to any act, from its conformity or non-conformity with rational nature itself, that

---

union of free men, associated for the sake of enjoying law and common utility." *J.B.P.*, 1.1.14.1: "Est autem civitas coetus perfectus liberorum hominum, juris fruendi et communis utilitatis causa sociatus."

[25] "Peace" is nowhere defined. *Framework*, 101.

[26] *J.B.P.*, 1.1.2.1; "bellum status per vim certantium qua tales sunt." The definition includes private war, and excludes "justness" as an element in the definition. *J.B.P.*, 1.1.2.3. In both respects Grotius departs from the definition given by Gentili. "Bellum" is rendered by van Vollenhoven as "armed coercion." *Framework*, 115, 120, 157; see also *Schets*, 94; and Grotius, *Commentary on the Law of Prize and Booty*, 30 (Williams and Zeydel's trans.). "Jus belli" may mean either "jus ad bellum" or "jus in bello." *Prolegomena* 28 in *J.B.P.*; *J.B.P.*, 1.1.3.1.

[27] *J.B.P.*, 1.1.3.1: "Nam jus hic nihil aliud quam quod justum est significat . . . quod injustum non est. Est autem injustum quod naturae societatis ratione utentium repugnat." "Jus" also may mean a "legal right." *J.B.P.*, 1.1.4.–.

[28] *J.B.P.*, 1.1.9.1, 3.20.25.–; *Prolegomena* 57 in *J.B.P.*; Dumbauld, *Interim Measures of Protection in International Controversies*, 8; Dumbauld, "The Place of Philosophy in International Law," *loc. cit.*, 590, 592.

[29] *J.B.P.*, 1.1.9.2; *Nicomachean Ethics*, Bk. 5, c. 10.

moral turpitude or moral necessity inheres in it, and hence that such act has been prohibited or commanded by God the author of nature."[30]

In the Declaration of Independence, Jefferson speaks of "the Laws of Nature and of Nature's God." It seems that in this expression natural and divine law are united in a single concept, rather than sharply separated as in the treatise of Grotius.[31] The Dutch jurist proceeds to designate as divine law that portion of the category of volitional law which proceeds from God's will rather than from human will.[32] Natural law, as the term is used by Grotius, may also be called divine;[33] but it is immutable and cannot be changed by God himself.[34] God is bound to ordain what it commands or prohibits, for the acts with which it deals are mandatory or illicit per se.[35] On the other hand, the

[30] *J.B.P.*, 1.1.10.1: "Jus naturale est dictatum rectae rationis indicans, actui alicui, ex ejus convenientia aut disconvenientia cum ipsa natura rationali, inesse moralem turpitudinem aut necessitatem moralem, ac consequenter ab auctore naturae Deo talem actum aut vetari aut praecipi."

[31] Dumbauld, *The Declaration of Independence and What It Means Today*, 44–45. The expression "God of Nature" occurs also in Patrick Henry's Liberty or Death speech, and in *Blackstone's Commentaries*, I, 123. Jefferson may have wished to distinguish "Nature's God" from "Calvin's God." Jefferson to John Adams, April 11, 1823, *The Writings of Thomas Jefferson*, XV, 425 (Lipscomb and Bergh, eds.).

[32] *J.B.P.*, 1.1.15.1.   [33] *Ibid.*   [34] *J.B.P.*, 1.1.10.5.

[35] *J.B.P.*, 1.1.10.2: "Actus de quibus tale exstat dictatum, debiti sunt aut illiciti per se, atque ideo a Deo necessario praecepti aut vetiti intelliguntur: qua nota distat hoc jus non ab humano tantum jure, sed et a divino voluntario, quod non ea praecipit aut vetat, quae per se ac suapte natura aut debita sunt aut illicita, sed vetando illicita, praecipiendo debita facit." *J.B.P.*, 1.15.1.–: "Jus voluntarium divinum . . . ex voluntate divina ortum habet . . . non ideo id Deum velle, quia justum est, sed justum esse, id est jure debitum, quia Deus voluit."

acts which are commanded or prohibited by divine volitional law (*jus divinum voluntarium*) are not so commanded or prohibited because they are just or unjust; rather, they
become just or unjust only because God has so willed.[36]

Human volitional law (*jus voluntarium humanum*), the
other branch of the dichotomy into which volitional law
is divided, contains three subclassifications: civil law,[37] a
wider species, and a narrower species. The narrower species
embraces paternal precepts (*praecepta patria, dominica,
et si qua sunt similia*) and the like.[38] The wider species is
the law of nations (*jus gentium*), that is to say, that law
which has received obligatory force from the will of all
nations (or of many).[39]

By this threefold criterion (natural law, the law of nations, and volitional divine law) Grotius proceeds to treat
the topics of war and peace which constitute the subject
matter of his treatise.[40]

II.

The first question discussed is whether war is ever justified.[41] Against the excessive quietism of many estimable
Christian thinkers who hold it wrong to bear arms at all,[42]

[36] Grotius differs with those who say that the commands of God
do not go beyond the law of nature. *J.B.P.*, 1.2.6.2.

[37] For the definition of civil law, see note 24, above.

[38] *J.B.P.*, 1.1.14.1: "Est ergo hoc vel civile, vel latius patens, vel
arctius."

[39] *J.B.P.*, 1.1.14.1: "Jus gentium, id est quod gentium omnium
aut multarum voluntate vim obligandi accepit."

[40] *Prolegomena* 1, 41 in *J.B.P.* As previously noted, civil law is
outside the scope of his book. P. 61, above; see also *Schets*, 95–96.

[41] *Prolegomena* 33 in *J.B.P.*; *J.B.P.*, 1.2.1.–.

[42] *Prolegomena* 29 in *J.B.P.*

Grotius concludes that war is permitted by natural law,[43] the law of nations,[44] and volitional divine law as contained both in the Old[45] and New[46] Testaments. War is next distinguished into public, private, and mixed, and the legitimacy of each of these species of war is demonstrated.[47] Since public war may be waged only by authority of the holder of the sovereign power, Grotius then discusses sovereignty.[48] Neither private nor public persons may lawfully wage war against their superiors, according to Grotius; although unquestionably orders given in violation of natural or divine law must not be obeyed.[49] The limited scope of the exceptions which Grotius allows to this duty of nonresistance to rulers[50] may explain why at the time of the American Revolution the doctrines of Vattel were more popular in the United States than those of Grotius, if such a preference in fact existed.[51]

[43] *J.B.P.*, 1.2.4.1, 1.5.1.–.
[44] *J.B.P.*, 1.2.4.2.
[45] *J.B.P.*, 1.2.5.10.
[46] *J.B.P.*, 1.2.7.1.
[47] *J.B.P.*, 1.3.1.1, 1.3.1.2, 1.3.3.3, 1.3.4.1, 1.3.5.7, 1.4.1.1.
[48] *J.B.P.*, 1.3.6–24.–.
[49] *J.B.P.*, 1.4.1.3, 1.4.2.1, 1.4.6.1, 1.3.9.1.
[50] *J.B.P.*, 1.4.8–14.–. "His definition of the cases in which resistance is justified is so narrow that it may be doubted whether any case but that of the Netherlands ever fell within it." Figgis, *Studies of Political Thought from Gerson to Grotius*, 185. The Dutch historian Fruin observes that when he wrote *De Jure Praedae* Grotius thought of himself as a citizen of a republic which had heroically won its liberty in a successful rebellion; whereas when he wrote *De Jure Belli ac Pacis* his status was that of a ruler banished by an uprising against the legitimate government. Robert J. Fruin, *Verspreide Geschriften*, III, 59.
[51] *Writings*, I, 430. See p. 30, above. Lipscomb and Bergh, *The Writings of Thomas Jefferson*, III, 237, shows an instance where Jefferson preferred Grotius over Vattel. Grotius rejected the view

In Book II Grotius turns to the problem of what constitutes just cause for war and finds that nothing but an injury
furnishes such cause.[52] Hence there may be as many just
causes of war as there are types of injury. Grotius draws the
parallel, previously noted,[53] between war and judicial remedies.[54] From the maxim *ubi jus ibi remedium*[55] (wherever
there is a right there is a remedy), it follows that in order to
determine the circumstances under which the remedy of
armed coercion may be pursued, it is necessary for Grotius
to review the entire repertory of substantive legal rights
which, under the system of law with which he is concerned,
are enjoyed by potential belligerents. Each of such substantive rights, if violated, may give rise to a just cause of war
when law enforcement by armed coercion is the only procedural remedy available to the injured party.[56]

---

that sovereignty everywhere belongs to the people and that all government exists for the sake of the governed, not the rulers. *J.B.P.*,
1.3.8.1, 1.3.8.14. He also denied that liberty was a just cause of
war. *J.B.P.*, 2.22.11.–. Vattel was relied on by the colonists to show
that their independence was justified by violation of fundamental
law by the British. Dumbauld, *The Declaration of Independence
and What It Means Today*, 139.

[52] *Prolegomena* 34 in *J.B.P.*; *J.B.P.*, 2.1.1.4: "Causa justa belli
suscipiendi nulla esse alia potest nisi injuria."

[53] See pp. 33, 59–60, above.

[54] *J.B.P.*, 2.1.2.1: "Ac plane quot actionum forensium sunt fontes,
totidem sunt belli: nam ubi judicia deficiunt incipit bellum." See
also *Framework*, 29; *Schets*, 95. See p. 33, above.

[55] Dumbauld, *Interim Measures of Protection in International
Controversies*, 12.

[56] This remedy takes three forms: defense, recovery of property,
and punishment. *J.B.P.*, 2.1.2.2. The first two types are combined
by van Vollenhoven, whose analysis specifies only: (1) civil redress;
and (2) punishment of criminal wrongs. *Framework*, 66, 70. Cf.
De Jure Praedae: "Quid jus sit vidimus: unde injuria etiam noscitur."
D.J.P., 30; *L.P.B.*, 30.

Het Huis te LOEVESTEIN

A. Rademaker fecit

LOEVESTEIN CASTLE IN THE YEAR OF GROTIUS' ESCAPE

*Engraving
by A. Rademaker*

*From the private collection
of Dr. B. L. Meulenbroek*

156

1636.

A. Rademaker fecit   Het Huis te LOEVESTEIN

LOEVESTEIN CASTLE IN 1636

Engraving
by A. Rademaker

From the private collection
of Dr. B. L. Meulenbroek

The scheme which Grotius adopted for his discussion of this catalogue of substantive rights was taken from the Roman civil law.[57] His treatment of persons, things, obligations, contracts, delicts, crimes, and the like, in chapters 2–17 of Book II, is reminiscent of the topics familiar since Justinian's *Corpus Juris Civilis*. This Romanistic material is supplemented in chapters 18 and 19 by material drawn from the law of nations (*jus illud gentium quod voluntarium dicimus*) regarding the right of embassy and of sepulture. Following this treatment of the law of peace apart from penalties, comes chapter 20, dealing with punishment, which is the longest in the book. It is considered by van Vollenhoven as the climax and essence of Grotian doctrine.[58]

Book II concludes[59] with several chapters dealing with subsidiary and incidental matters. Though cognizant that unjust causes of war can be recognized from the preceding discussion of just causes, in the same manner as crookedness will be disclosed by its deviation from a straight line,[60]

[57] *Framework*, 103. The same scheme was followed by Blackstone in his *Commentaries on the Laws of England*. As a youth Grotius had paraphrased in verse part of the *Corpus Juris* (Inst., II, i, "de rerum divisione & acquirendo earum dominio"). *Bibliographie*, 2, 87. In 1642 he published a collection of comments on the *Corpus Juris*, his *Florum Sparsio ad Jus Justinianeum*. See pp. 128–30, 165, below.

[58] See p. 60, above. Chapter 21 continues the subject of punishment, dealing with vicarious responsibility for the acts of others. Akin to this chapter is the theological tract published by Grotius in 1617 to show that Arminian views on the atonement were not Socinian: *Defensio fidei catholicae de satisfactione Christi Adversus Faustum Socinum Senensem*. See *Schets*, 63.

[59] Material in *J.B.P.*, 3.9.4.1–3, relating to *postliminium* in peacetime, as van Vollenhoven observes, logically belongs in Book 2. *Framework*, 106.

[60] *J.B.P.*, 2.22.4.–.

THE LIFE AND LEGAL WRITINGS OF HUGO GROTIUS

Grotius nevertheless for the sake of clearness adds chapter 22 enumerating unjust causes of war. These include "preventive" war when the strength of a rival nation is increasing, desire for autonomy or subjugation of others,[61] and various religious motives. Chapter 23 treats doubtful causes of war and advises that when opinions are balanced, preference should be given to peace[62] and alternatives explored such as conference and arbitration.[63] Chapter 24 is an admonition against going to war rashly, even for just causes. Chapter 25 treats of protection by war of the interests of others, such as allies, subjects, or friends. Grotius holds that humanity itself is a sufficient warrant for war, or the rescuing of an oppressed people from manifest wrongs by their ruler.[64] The final chapter in Book II deals with the situation of those who are not their own masters but are subject to the authority of another. Grotius declares it is their duty to abstain from war if they are certain that the cause of war is unjust,[65] and he urges recognition of the rights of conscientious objectors.[66]

Book III deals with the "law of war" (*jus in bello*) as understood in modern international law, as dealt with at the Hague Peace Conferences of 1899 and 1907, and in the rules which emanated therefrom regulating the methods of warfare. Grotius here continues to apply his threefold

[61] Likewise in *De Jure Praedae* Grotius says that neither domination nor liberty is a just cause for war. D.J.P., 70; L.P.B., 69.

[62] J.B.P., 2.23.6.–.

[63] J.B.P., 2.23.7–8.–.

[64] J.B.P., 2.25.6.–, 2.25.8.–. According to Grotius, it would have been wrong for Americans to resist British rule at the time of the Revolution, but permissible for the French to come to our assistance. J.B.P., 2.25.8.3. See note 51, above.

[65] J.B.P., 2.26.3.1. See also note 49, above.

[66] J.B.P., 2.26.5.1–2.

criterion of natural law, the law of nations, and divine volitional law in order to determine what is lawful in war.[67] The primary rule of natural law is that whatever is necessary is lawful.[68] The use of stratagems and deceit is considered, but a firm stand is taken against violation of oaths and promises.[69]

Coming to what the law of nations permits in war, Grotius concludes that the subjects of a ruler who does an injury are liable in their person and property to reprisals.[70] A solemn declaration of war is required by the law of nations, but not by the law of nature.[71] Enemies may be slain anywhere except in neutral territory.[72] Poison is prohibited, however, by the law of nations.[73] Assassination is permissible provided it entails no breach of faith.[74] Grotius favors the rule forbidding rape.[75] Destruction of property, and capture, are permitted.[76] The rule that enemy ships make enemy goods is merely a rebuttable presumption, not a settled rule of the law of nations.[77] Contrary to the common view, Grotius asserts that when property is captured by soldiers in their official capacity, the booty belongs to the

[67] *Prolegomena* 35 in *J.B.P.*; *J.B.P.*, 3.1.1.–. "quid quantumque in bello liceat, et quibus modis." The rules laid down by Grotius in Book 3 had considerable influence on state practice. *Writings*, I, 479.
[68] *J.B.P.*, 3.1.2.1.
[69] *J.B.P.*, 3.1.18–19.–.
[70] *J.B.P.*, 3.2.5.2, 3.2.7.2.
[71] *J.B.P.*, 3.3.6.1.
[72] *J.B.P.*, 3.4.8.2.
[73] *J.B.P.*, 3.4.14.1.
[74] *J.B.P.*, 3.4.18.1.
[75] *J.B.P.*, 3.4.19.2.
[76] *J.B.P.*, 3.5.1.–, 3.6.2.1.
[77] *J.B.P.*, 3.6.6.–.

state (if its civil law does not provide differently), and it may transfer it to whom it will.[78]

Regarding prisoners of war, slavery was introduced by the law of nations. Among Christians this rule has been changed.[79] Likewise rules of *postliminium*, treating the conditions under which persons or property taken in war regain their former status on return to their own nation, are obsolete among Christians.[80]

Chapters 10–16 of Book III qualify the belligerent rights previously discussed by setting up admonitions (*monita*) and mitigations (*temperamenta*) in accordance with a distinction between what is lawful merely because it may be done with impunity and what is lawful in the sense of right or just. This higher standard Grotius calls "internal justice." He praises the virtues of honor, moderation, and magnanimity. The lives of women, children, the aged, and those whose way of life is remote from warfare (such as priests, scholars, farmers, tradesmen) may be properly spared.[81] Unnecessary destruction of property is also imprudent.[82] Charity with regard to capture and kind treatment of prison-

[78] *J.B.P.*, 3.6.14.1. The view of Grotius represents the practice followed by the States of Holland in the case of the *Catharina*, which furnished the occasion for writing *De Jure Praedae*. Molhuysen, "Over Grotius' De Jure Praedae Commentarius," *loc. cit.*, 275–82; Fruin, "An Unpublished Work of Hugo Grotius's," *loc. cit.*, 25.

[79] *J.B.P.*, 3.7.5.1, 3.7.9.1.

[80] *J.B.P.*, 3.9.19.1.

[81] *J.B.P.*, 3.11.9–13.–. Compare the provisions of the treaty with Prussia negotiated by Franklin, Adams, and Jefferson, *The Works of Thomas Jefferson*, IV, 354 (Ford ed.); also The Paquete Habana, 175 U.S. 677 (1900); and *D.J.P.*, 109, *L.P.B.*, 110.

[82] *J.B.P.*, 3.12.8.1. Grotius here makes the often-quoted remark: "Virtue, so little esteemed in this age, should pardon me if, when for herself she is spurned, I make her sought on account of her utility."

ers of war are likewise enjoined.[83] Moderation is also
urged[84] with respect to exercise of the right to subjugate a
whole people and extinguish a state.[85] Retention of their
government by the conquered people is often a measure
indicated by prudence as well as humanity.[86]

Chapter 17 deals with nonparticipants in a war (*de his
qui in bello medii sunt*). Grotius does not use the word
"neutrals." In his view they were not neutral in the conflict but were under a duty to do nothing to hinder the
party waging a just war or to aid the culprit.[87] Chapter 18
considers the use of privateers.[88] The remaining seven chapters of Book III discuss the topic of good faith. The book
ends with an eloquent admonition to the rulers of nations
to cherish good faith and to cultivate peace:

> For by faith is not only every commonwealth held
> together, as Cicero says, but also that greater society of
> nations. . . .
> May God (who alone can do so) write these things
> in the hearts of those in whose hands are the affairs of
> Christendom, and endue them with a mind understand-
> ing divine and human law, and which may always reflect

[83] *J.B.P.*, 3.13.4.1, 3.14.2.3.

[84] *J.B.P.*, 3.15.2.1, 3.15.4.1.

[85] Regarding this belligerent right, see *J.B.P.*, 3.8.1.1, 3.8.2.1.

[86] *J.B.P.*, 3.15.7.1. Moderation is also urged with respect to things
to which *postliminium* does not apply. *J.B.P.*, 3.16.1.1–2. "What is
captured in an unjust war is to be restored . . . in internal justice,
an unjust war does not differ from a robbery."

[87] *J.B.P.*, 3.17.3.1. See p. 60, above.

[88] *J.B.P.*, 3.18.1–2.–. See *Schets*, 39, and *J.B.P.*, 2.17.20.– regarding
a question on this subject dealt with by Grotius while he was *Advocaat-Fiscaal* of Holland.

that it has been called to the ministry of ruling men, a creature most dear to God.[89]

III.

In the *Prolegomena* prefacing his book, Grotius explains the nature and purpose of his work. He observes that the civil law (both Roman and that of each nation) has often been the subject of textbooks and commentaries but that few writers have touched upon, and none has treated in a comprehensive and orderly manner, "that law which governs among several peoples or the rulers of peoples." Yet it is of importance to the human race that that be done.[90]

International law is thus the principal theme of his treatise although, as has been noted above,[91] the legal system which Grotius expounds goes beyond interstate relations and (while excluding civil law) is in reality a universal law binding all mankind. Even in the time of Grotius there were those who denied the existence of international law. Long before the Austinians and pragmatists it was said that

[89] *J.P.B.*, 3.25.1.–, 3.25.8.–. In chapter 6 (*De fide et perfidia*) of Book 3 of a work, *Parallelon Rerumpublicarum*, comparing the Athenian, Roman, and Batavian commonwealths, which he wrote in 1601 or 1602 but never published, Grotius emphasized the importance of good faith, thus foreshadowing the basic doctrine contained in *De Jure Belli ac Pacis*. Van Eysinga, "Het oudste bekende geschrift van de Groot over Volkenrecht," *loc. cit.*, 463. It is also curious that in the first diplomatic mission of Grotius at the age of fifteen his countrymen were vainly seeking to make Henry IV of France live up to a treaty of 1596 prohibiting separate peace with Spain. Likewise the first task of Grotius as Swedish ambassador in 1635 was to urge France to go to war. *Schets*, 12–13, 108–10.

[90] *Prolegomena* 1 in *J.B.P.* See note 22, above.

[91] Pp. 55, 59, 61, above. See also van Eysinga, "De beteekenis van de Groot voor het internationale recht," *loc. cit.*, 76, 78.

this branch of law was only an empty name.[92] The controversies between kings and peoples commonly lead to war, and war is far removed from any law.

Controverting this common opinion, Grotius declares that war itself is an instrumentality of law. Far from admitting that in war all legal rights cease, Grotius asserts that war is not to be undertaken except for the enforcement of law, nor is it to be waged, when undertaken, except within the limitations prescribed by law and good faith.[93] He held with the utmost certainty that there was a law among peoples which was in force with respect to resort to war and with respect to conduct of war.[94]

The maxim *inter arma silent leges* was treated by Grotius as applicable only to the sphere of civil law. In warfare there were in force between enemies those unwritten laws "which nature dictates or the consensus of nations has established."[95] For the law of nature Grotius found a basis in human nature.[96] This foundation would remain firm

[92] *Prolegomena* 3 in *J.B.P.*: "et nostro seculo non desunt et olim non defuerunt qui hanc juris partem ita contemnerent, quasi nihil ejus praeter inane nomen existeret."

[93] *Prolegomena* 25 in *J.B.P.* See pp. 43, 59–60, above. See also *Prolegomena* 28 in *J.B.P.* Van Eysinga, "De beteekenis van de Groot voor het internationale recht," *loc. cit.*, 76, 78.

[94] *Prolegomena* 28 in *J.B.P.*: "Ego cum ob eas quas jam dixi, rationes, compertissimum haberem, esse aliquod inter populos jus commune, quod et ad bella, et in bellis valeret, cur de eo instituerem scriptionem, causas habui multas ac graves."

[95] *Prolegomena* 26 in *J.B.P.*: "ea quae natura dictat, aut gentium consensus constituit."

[96] *Prolegomena* 6 in *J.B.P.*: "Inter haec autem quae homini sunt propria, est appetitus societatis, id est communitatis, non qualiscunque, sed tranquillae, et pro sui intellectus modo ordinatae, cum his qui sunt generis." See also *Prolegomena* 8–9 in *J.B.P.* In *Prolegomena* 16 he says: "Naturalis juris mater est ipsa humana natura . . . civilis vero juris mater est ipsa ex consensu obligatio, quae . . . ex naturali

even if it should wickedly be supposed that God does not exist or takes no concern in human affairs.[97] The law of nations, Grotius states, was established for the utility of mankind as a whole by the consent of all (or most) nations.[98] Evidence of such consent is to be gathered from history.[99] He considered it very important to distinguish clearly between the law of nature and the law of nations[100] and

---

jure vim suam [habet]." Civil law is based upon consent, which natural law makes binding by the rule *pacta sunt servanda*. *Prolegomena* 15 in *J.B.P.*: "cum juris naturae sit stare pactis . . . ab hoc ipso fonte jura civilia fluxerunt." Regarding the influence of the social-compact philosophy in American political theory, see Dumbauld, *The Declaration of Independence and What It Means Today*, 31, 69–74, 121. See p. 81, below.

[97] *Prolegomena* 11 in *J.B.P.*: "Et haec quidem quae jam diximus, locum aliquem haberent etiamsi daremus, quod sine summo scelere dari nequit, non esse Deum, aut non curari ab eo negotia humana." Grotius regarded the will of God as another source of law. *Prolegomena* 12 in *J.B.P.* Regarding the universality of the binding force of law in the view of Grotius, see *Writings*, I, 411.

[98] *Prolegomena* 17 in *J.B.P.*: "Sed sicut cujusque civitatis jura utilitatem suae civitatis respiciunt, ita inter civitates aut omnes aut plerasque ex consensu jura quaedam nasci potuerunt, et nata apparet, quae utilitatem respicerent non coetuum singulorum, sed magnae illius universitatis. Et hoc jus est quod gentium dicitur, quoties id nomen a jure naturali distinguimus."

[99] *Prolegomena* 46 in *J.B.P.*

[100] *Prolegomena* 30 in *J.B.P.* There is no substantial difference between the systems of definitions in the *De Jure Belli ac Pacis* and in the *De Jure Praedae* though in the latter he speaks of "primary" and "secondary" law of nations, the first being equivalent to the law of nature, and the second being based on consent. Grotius, *Commentary on the Law of Prize and Booty*, 12, 26 (Williams and Zeydel's trans.). Regarding the philosophy of law held by Grotius, see Hugo Fortuin, *De natuurrechtelijke grondslagen van de Groot's volkenrecht*; H. Bertens, *Hugo de Groot en zijn Rechtsphilosophie*; and Gustav Hartenstein, *Darstellung der Rechtsphilosophie des Hugo Grotius*.

claimed to have done so,[101] although other writers, in his opinion, had treated this matter with hopeless confusion.[102]

Being certain of the existence of this twofold law of war (*jus ad bellum* and *in bello*) which rested on a threefold foundation (*jus naturae, gentium,* and *divinum voluntarium*), Grotius was impelled to write his book because of the shameful license and lawlessness which he beheld in the Christian world of his day.[103] The sight of such outrages caused many estimable thinkers to conclude, erroneously, that a Christian must abstain entirely from military activities. Grotius regarded it as important to point out, with discriminating exactitude, the fallacy of both extreme views: the one which thought that everything was allowable, and the other which thought that nothing was.[104] The wars of that era were not exclusively international in the modern sense; Grotius meant the rules he formulated to apply to all warfare, to all mankind.[105] Merely from the standpoint of selfish advantage, he stressed the benefits of law observance by individuals and nations.[106] No nation is so strong that it may not sometime need the aid of others.[107]

His purpose thus being to move the hearts of peoples and their rulers, Grotius molded the form and style of his

101 *Prolegomena* 41 in *J.B.P.*
102 *Prolegomena* 37, 40, 53 in *J.B.P.*
103 *Prolegomena* 28 in *J.B.P.*: "Videbam per Christianum orbem, vel barbaris gentibus pudendam bellandi licentiam: levibus aut nullis de causis ad arma procurri, quibus semel sumtis nullam jam divini, nullam humani juris reverentiam, plane quasi uno edicto ad omnia scelera emisso furore." See also *Bibliographie,* 226.
104 *Prolegomena* 29 in *J.B.P.*
105 *Writings,* I, 393.
106 *Prolegomena* 18 in *J.B.P.*
107 *Prolegomena* 22 in *J.B.P.*

THE LIFE AND LEGAL WRITINGS OF HUGO GROTIUS

treatise accordingly. He did not write a dry textbook
for law students but employed the ornaments of eloquence and wit.[108] Above all, he aimed at clearness and
conciseness, wishing his work to be useful to practical men
of affairs.[109] He refrained from discussion of political matters and from allusion to current controversies of his day.[110]
His examples and illustrations were derived from ancient
history. Classical antiquity and Biblical writers are drawn
on copiously.[111] Poets and orators are quoted, mostly for
the sake of adornment and elegance.[112] His erudition seems
somewhat excessive and distracting to a modern reader.[113]
But Grotius desired to be complete and comprehensive,
esteeming lack of historical documentation (from which
alone the rules of the law of nations can be proved)[114] to be
the chief fault of previous writers.[115]

In concluding the *Prolegomena*, Grotius wrote: "And
now, if anything here has been said by me which is at vari-
ance with piety, good morals, holy scriptures, the consensus

[108] *Framework*, 27–28; *Writings*, I, 378, 390, 393, 417; *Prolegomena*, 47, 60 in J.B.P.

[109] *Prolegomena* 56, 59 in J.B.P.

[110] *Prolegomena* 57, 58 in J.B.P. Grotius seldom deviated from
this practice until the editions of 1642 and 1646 in which he added
references to recent events. *Framework*, 23.

[111] *Prolegomena* 40, 46, 48 in J.B.P.

[112] *Prolegomena* 47 in J.B.P. The extent of the activities of Gro-
tius himself as a poet has recently been emphasized by Judge W. J.
M. van Eysinga in *American Journal of International Law*, Vol.
XLV (1951), 810. See also E. H. Bodkin, "The Minor Poetry of
Hugo Grotius," *Transactions of Grotius Society*, Vol. XIII (1928),
95–128; and *Writings*, I, 231–86.

[113] *Writings*, I, 391; *Framework*, 20.

[114] *Prolegomena* 46 in J.B.P. Such data are also esteemed by
Grotius as useful in proving the law of nature. See also *Prolegomena*
40 in J.B.P.

[115] *Prolegomena* 38, 39 in J.B.P.

of the Christian church, or any truth, let it be as if not said."[116]

The extent to which Grotius drew from a multitude of literary sources is not surprising in view of his amazing range of interests as a scholar. The erudite exile of forty-two who gave to the world his masterpiece at Paris in 1625 was no novice in the world of letters.[117] Not without reason was he called "the wonder of Holland" and the "jurisconsult of humankind."

IV.

In his use of Roman civil law and the Bible as a means

[116] *Prolegomena* 61 in *J.B.P.*: "Et jam nunc adeo, si quid hic pietati, si quid bonis moribus, si quid sacris litteris, si quid Ecclesiae Christianae consensui, si quid ulli veritati dissentaneum a me dictum est, id nec dictum esto."

[117] Before 1625, besides editing ancient texts, Grotius had versified part of the Roman *Corpus Juris*, had written his earlier work on international law, *Parallelon Rerumpublicarum* (published by Johan Meerman two centuries later in 1801–1803), his *De Jure Praedae*, of which one famous chapter on freedom of the seas was separately published in 1609, his celebrated *Introduction to the Jurisprudence of Holland*, and its companion-piece in the field of Dutch public law, the *Apologeticus*, in which he justified his course in the constitutional conflicts leading to his arrest and exile. A collection of poems published in 1617, his treatise on the atonement in the same year, his widely read work on the truth of the Christian religion, his *Annotations* on Bible passages (completed in later life and published in 1641), a catechism on baptism for his daughter Cornelia, a book of hymns, two of his three plays (*Adamus Exul* and *Christus Patiens*; *Sophompaneas* dates from 1635), two works on the history of Holland (*De Antiquitate Reipublicae Batavicae* [1610], *Chronicon Hollandiae* [1617]), and several treatises (including the posthumously published *De imperio summarum potestatum circa sacra*) defending the action of the States of Holland in the matter of religion had also served to establish his reputation in the republic of letters.

for giving content to what he described as the law of nature, Grotius did not depart greatly from medieval juristic theory. Resemblances are noticeable, for example, between the system of Grotius and the teachings of John of Salisbury, who wrote in the middle of the twelfth century before the revival of learning had familiarized western thought with Aristotle's writings and other aspects of classical antiquity. In his translation of the *Policraticus*, John Dickinson writes:

> It has become a historical commonplace that mediaeval thought was dominated by the conception of a body of law existing independently of the authority of any government and to which all positive law must conform and to which government no less than individuals owed obedience. . . .
>
> The identification of the "higher law" with the "law of God" as embodied in the scriptures, and the belief that its provisions were directly reproduced in existing texts of the Roman law, eliminated for thinkers of the twelfth century one of the cardinal difficulties which beset the doctrine of a "higher law" when it appears in the supremacy of a "law of nature,"—the difficulty, namely, of identifying any specific rules or precepts as belonging to this law. . . .
>
> The conception of a "higher law" had two other consequences which tended to retard the organization of effective government. On the one hand, it opened the door wide to individual resistance of governmental power. . . . Even the soldier, according to John of Salisbury, must resist the commands of his superior officer in cases where these transcend the "higher law." The result of this conception was at once to promote the natural mediaeval proclivity toward private war which expressed itself in the practical workings of feudalism and on the other hand to

give to such war that character of a struggle for legal rights which Stubbs has cited as one of the most character- istic features of mediaeval history.

In the second place . . . it produced a tendency toward political "quietism." . . . On this view, if government acted illegally it disobeyed God and God might very well be trusted to punish violations of His own law. If He did not do so, it must be because He had some hidden purpose of His own to further, perchance the punish- ment of an unfaithful people, by permitting them to be oppressed by the illegal acts of an unjust king. Under such circumstances men would be impiously presump- tuous if they undertook to . . . throw off the tyranny to which God wished them to be subjected for their sins. This view is very strong in John of Salisbury.[118]

Parallels to these aspects of medieval legal thinking can be found in Grotius, as has been shown by the analysis of his treatise hereinabove.

Yet the significance of Grotius lies in the fact that his work gave content and impetus to the nascent science of

[118] *The Statesman's Book of John of Salisbury*, xxviii, xxxiv, xxx–xxxi (1927). This difficulty besets all "natural law" philosophy. Dumbauld, "Judicial Review and Popular Sovereignty," *loc. cit.*, 204–205. Such theory proves unworkable except when there is a general unanimity or agreement as to the underlying moral basis or religious foundation. Such a consensus was available when Grotius wrote but is not attainable under the present-day conditions of ideological controversy. Arthur Nussbaum, "Just War—A Legal Concept?," *Michigan Law Review*, Vol. XLII, No. 3 (Dec., 1943), 453, 474–79. Even St. Paul in 1 Cor. 11:14 when appealing to the Corinthians to judge for themselves what "nature itself" teaches, "applies the concept to the rather trivial question of wearing the hair long or short, actually a matter of social convention. Even an apostle is not exempt from the human tendency to mistake convention and prejudice for the law of nature." Millar Burrows, *An Outline of Bibli- cal Theology*, 38. See also J.B.P., 2.20.41.–.

international law. That branch of jurisprudence (understood as the body of law which regulates the mutual relations of independent sovereign states) did not, and could not, come into being until the establishment of the modern state-system which after the Reformation replaced the earlier legal unity of Christendom under the Papacy and Holy Roman Empire.[119] The treatise of Grotius, published in 1625, furnished the intellectual foundation for the political development which achieved definitive recognition at the close of the Thirty Years' War in 1648. As James Bryce writes:

When by the Peace of Westphalia a crowd of petty principalities were recognized as practically independent states, the need of a body of rules to regulate their relations and intercourse became pressing. Such a code (if one may call it by that name) Grotius and his successors compiled out of the principles which they found in the Roman law, then the private law of Germanic countries, thus laying the foundation whereon the system of international jurisprudence has been built up during the last three centuries.[120]

The threefold basis of the Grotian system (*jus naturae, gentium,* and *divinum voluntarium*) served to support the structure of rules binding upon separate national states

[119] James L. Brierly, *The Law of Nations,* 9; Figgis, *Studies of Political Thought from Gerson to Grotius,* 17, 189–90. The term "international law" seems to have been coined by Jeremy Bentham, *An Introduction to the Principles of Morals and Legislation,* 326.

[120] James Bryce, *The Holy Roman Empire,* 436. See also Figgis, *Studies of Political Thought from Gerson to Grotius,* 186, and Angelo P. Sereni, *The Italian Conception of International Law,* 15, 58, 66, 120.

until later thinkers perceived that these rules could be rested upon a completely positivistic *jus gentium* derived exclusively from a single maxim of natural law, *pacta sunt servanda*.[121] Yet the historical tradition of this body of law, going back through Grotius to the old unity of Christendom, gave a specific character and individuality to the growing system of jurisprudence which regulated the concerns of sovereign states. Thus the community of nations was not regarded as an atomistic aggregation of separate units having no duties *inter sese*. At the same time, international law was not an empty, generalized body of law applicable to the relations of any or all powers not recognizing a common earthly superior.[122] What we now think of as international law does not include such systems of interstate law or *jus inter potestates* as may have prevailed among independent political units in ancient Greek, Assyrian, Babylonian, Egyptian, or Chinese history.[123] Similarly, the body of rules

[121] "The fundamental basis of the whole system of Grotius is the claim that men are in a society bound together by a natural law which makes promises binding." Figgis, *Studies of Political Thought from Gerson to Grotius*, 186; Alfred Verdross, *Die Verfassung der Völkerrechtsgemeinschaft*, 27–28. On the same basis was built the social-contract theory of Locke and the structure of political liberty recognized under English constitutional law. Dumbauld, *The Declaration of Independence and What It Means Today*, 49, 69–74.

[122] The highly esteemed Italian jurist Dionisio Anzilotti, late president-judge of the Permanent Court of International Justice, took the rule *pacta sunt servanda* as the fundamental norm of international law and regarded any *jus inter potestates* whose binding force rests on that rule as part of international law. Dumbauld, "The Place of Philosophy in International Law," *loc. cit.*, 590, 601. But this would make the internal civil or constitutional law of a single state, derived from the same maxim in accordance with Locke's social-contract theory, also a part of international law.

[123] Alfred Verdross, *Völkerrecht*, 5. See also, regarding *jus inter potestates*, Verdross, *Die Verfassung der Völkerrechtsgemeinschaft*, 116–18.

81

applied (in the absence of specific provisions of constitutional law) by a judicial tribunal empowered to decide disputes between the component states of a federal union is not, strictly speaking, international law, but is a special variety of municipal or constitutional law.[124] Likewise, from a theoretical standpoint, if a single world government were established with powers to repress resort to war by individual nations and to adjudicate all controversies among them, the law then in force would no longer be international law in the conventional sense but the internal or municipal law of the new international commonwealth or "superstate."[125] Yet even there the law of which Grotius so feelingly discoursed in his magistral treatise would not be out of place.

[124] Dumbauld, *Interim Measures of Protection in International Controversies*, 82.

[125] Burckhardt, *Die Unvollkommenheit des Völkerrechts*, 3; "The Place of Philosophy in International Law," *loc. cit.*, 590, 600; Williams, Book Review, *Harvard Law Review*, Vol. XLV (1931), 225, 227; Verdross, *Völkerrecht*, 48.

Defense of the Lawful Government
of Holland
Apologeticus

Among the prominent Frenchmen with whom the exiled Dutch jurist Hugo Grotius was intimately associated in Paris, following his spectacular escape from the castle of Loevestein in 1621,[1] was Pierre Jeannin, one of the ministers of King Louis XIII. At the suggestion of Jeannin, Grotius began to write—while the events were fresh in his mind—a defense of his own good name and of the legality of the conduct in which he had engaged as an official of the government of Holland.[2] Accordingly, Grotius asked his brother-in-law, Nicholas van Reigersberch, to send him papers needed for that purpose. He also sought pertinent data from other persons having information on the subject. In September, 1621, his wife arrived in Paris, bringing needed documents. By October, Grotius was at work on the book.[3]

[1] See p. 13, above.

[2] *Historie*, I, 280. By "Holland" is meant, not the whole United Netherlands, but the Province of Holland and West Friesland, of which Grotius was a high official at the time of his arrest in 1618. See p. 16, above.

[3] H. C. Rogge, "De 'Verantwoordingh' van Hugo de Groot," *Bijdragen voor Vaderlandsche Geschiedenis en Oudheidkunde* (derde reeks), Vol. VII (1892), 89, 92, 98, 100 [hereinafter cited as Rogge]. This article gives a good account of the circumstances sur-

Early in February, 1622, Grotius completed a draft of this work in Dutch. He sent the manuscript to his friend du Maurier, the French ambassador in the Netherlands, in order that its accuracy might be checked by friends familiar with the laws and customs of Holland.[4] Meanwhile, Grotius undertook the preparation of a translation into Latin. Some who read the work doubted the advisability of its publication, fearing that it would merely revive old hatreds —to the detriment of the author and his family—by emphasizing truths that were distasteful to the rulers of the Netherlands.[5] Others urged that silence would be construed as an admission of guilt of the charges for which he had been imprisoned, and that for the sake of protecting his own good name Grotius must demonstrate his innocence and the illegality of the sentence of the tribunal which had condemned him.

After Grotius had decided to publish the book, Dutch authorities, through intercepted letters, discovered the fact that it was being printed in Amsterdam. A search of the printer's house resulted in seizure of material valued at 400 florins. Grotius' brother Willem was interrogated and kept in jail for several days, but proved that he had delivered the

---

rounding the writing and publication of the book, with references to Grotius' correspondence and other documents.

[4] Rogge, 101–102; *Historie*, I, 287. In the preface to his celebrated treatise on private law written during his confinement at Loevestein, Grotius likewise lamented his lack of opportunity for discussion with other legal experts. See p. 129, below.

[5] ". . . vrezende dat d'ontdekte waerheit te veel haets zou baeren of den ouden haet te zeer vermeerderen, tot nadeel van den Schryver, en de zynen." *Historie*, I, 287. Grotius was willing to soften the wording, but not the substance, of what he had written. Rogge, 103, 105. De Haan, a codefendant with Grotius, thought that the *Defense* did not criticize Prince Maurits severely enough. Rogge, 125–26.

manuscript a month previously to an emissary of the author and had taken a receipt. He declared that he knew nothing about plans for printing it, although a list of corrections to be made was in his possession.[6]

Although publication at Amsterdam was frustrated, the book was brought out at Hoorn in November, 1622, by Isaak Willemszoon Verbeek under the title *Verantwoordingh van de Vvettelijcke Regieringh van Hollandt Ende West-Vrieslandt, Mitsgaders Eenigher nabuyrighe Provincien sulcks die Was voor de veranderingh ghevallen in den Jare xvj^{c.} en xviij.*[7] Meanwhile a month earlier the Latin version, entitled *Apologeticvs eorvm qvi Hollandiae Vvestfrisiaeqve et vicinis quibusdam nationibus ex legibus praefuerunt ante mutationem quae evenit anno MDCXVIII,*[8] had appeared in Paris, with privilege from the king, printed by Nicholas Buon (the same publisher who three years later issued *De Jure Belli ac Pacis*).[9]

[6] Rogge, 110–16, 127–34; *Historie*, I, 288–91.

[7] Rogge, 117. I have used the copy in the Harvard Law School Library. The title may be translated: "Defense of the Lawful Government of Holland and West Friesland, together with some Neighboring Provinces, as it was before the Change Occurring in 1618." [Hereinafter cited as *Verantwoordingh.*] The imprint reads:

> Accordeert met het Latyn, ghedruckt
> TOT PARYS,
> Met Privilegie van den Coningh, 1622.

[8] This title may be translated: "Defense of those who according to law were in authority over Holland, West Friesland and certain neighboring nations before the change which came to pass in the year 1618." I have used the copy in the Harvard Law School Library. [Hereinafter cited as *Apologeticus.*]

[9] *Historie*, I, 293: ". . . eerst in Slachtmaendt uitgegeven, na dat de Latynsche vertaling ruim een maendt te vooren, met Privilegie des Konings, te Parys al was in 't licht gekomen." According to Rogge, 119, the Latin version came out three months before the Dutch. "Eerst drie manden na de Latinjnsche uitgave kwam de Neder-

The first edition in Latin was exhausted by August, 1625, but there was no reissue until Grotius' friend Lingelsheim caused a second edition to be published at Heidelberg in 1629. This was followed by those of Heidelberg, 1631; Paris, 1640; and Paris, 1665. Six slightly variant Dutch editions, the order of which it is not possible to determine, were printed, probably in 1623.[10] French and German translations, which Grotius hoped would be made of the *Defense*, never became a reality.[11] No English translation has ever been made.

The *Defense* was widely read in the Netherlands,[12] and led to a violent reaction on the part of the States-General. That body, on November 24, 1622, adopted a decree *(placcaet)* declaring the work to be a notorious, seditious, and scandalous libel and outlawing the author without benefit of the statute of limitations. It was also made punishable for anyone to print, distribute, possess, read, give to others for reading, bring in, or otherwise handle the book.[13]

---

landsche gereed." Rogge, 108, states that the Latin translation was copied by the beginning of April and went to press at the end of June. Printing of the Latin edition began in May or June, 1622, and was probably completed in August, according to ter Meulen et Diermanse, *Bibliographie*, 427.

10 Regarding the various editions of the *Defense*, see *Bibliographie*, 420–30, Item Nos. 872–84. Item No. 879 is reserved for a Dutch edition said to be in preparation by Fockema Andreae.

11 Rogge, 108, 119, 124.

12 *Historie*, I, 302. One great personage was reported to have lost his appetite for a tasty midday meal upon reading the book.

13 *Historie*, I, 303: ". . . een fameux, seditieux ende schandeleux Libel, den Autheur van dien strafbaer aen Lijf ende goedt . . . sonder dat eenigh verloop van Jaren hem hier af zal konnen bevrijden." A separate print of the *placcaet*, issued at The Hague in 1622 by the widow van Wouw who published the Inleidinge in 1631, is bound with the Harvard Law School Library's copy of the Verantwoordingh.

In response to a request by Grotius,[14] Louis XIII of France, on February 26, 1623, replied to the decree of the States-General by taking Grotius under the king's special protection and forbidding persons "of every quality, nation, or condition" from molesting or harming him.[15]

The book thus eventfully brought into being is regarded by competent Dutch jurists as an authoritative exposition of the public law of Holland in Grotius' day. It is thus a companion-piece to his widely used treatise on the private law of Holland.[16] Grotius himself so regarded it, for he never completed the portion of his *Introduction to the Jurisprudence of Holland* which would have dealt with public law, although he asserted that public law was more important than private law. Instead, he referred to his *Defense* for a treatment of that topic.[17]

The *Defense* was not so much a justification of his own conduct, Grotius pointed out in the preface, as it was a justification of the conduct of the lawful government of Holland.[18] Grotius was but a servant, his authority was that

[14] Rogge, 122–23; *Historie*, I, 306–10. Later to become famous as the "father of international law," Grotius in this request advanced an ingenious argument based upon private international law (or conflict of laws). He contended that since the book had been published in France, it could be criminal, if at all, only under the law of France, and that the author could be tried only in French courts. Since publication had been authorized by the privilege granted by the king, the Dutch decree was an infringement of the rights of France. *Historie*, I, 308–309.

[15] *Historie*, I, 310–11.

[16] *Schets*, 91. See also Wierdsma, *Politie en Justitie: Een Studie over Hollandschen Staatsbouw tijdens de Republiek*, xi, 7, 61, and de Vrankrijker, *De staatsleer van Hugo de Groot en zijn Nederlandsche tijdgenooten*, 6.

[17] See p. 133, below.

[18] *Schets*, 91.

of his masters.[19] At the time of his arrest by the States-General and his condemnation for *laesa majestas*, he insisted continually that all the acts laid to his charge were done by him solely under and by virtue of the authority of the government of Holland, whose public servant he was, and that the States-General had no jurisdiction to try him. He asserted that he was responsible only to his own masters.[20]

It was the misfortune of Grotius that a theological dispute about predestination became a constitutional conflict that touched the scope of the respective powers of the provincial and national governments.[21] Whatever the merits of the policy of tolerance preferred by the government of Holland and whatever the legal authority of that government to settle the question, the dogmatic Calvinism favored by the national government and backed by the troops of Prince Maurits was destined to prevail by reason of superior military and political strength.

Grotius' *Defense*, although it stands as a sound analysis of the constitutional law of Holland from a historical standpoint, has therefore been less influential[22] than his *Introduction* which treats private law topics, just as in the case of a later struggle against a victorious national government, the *post mortem* constitutional expositions of the defeated

[19] *Historie*, I, 294; *Verantwoordingh*, Preface, 3, 11. See also Rogge, 98.

[20] "Who art thou that judgest another man's servant? to his own master he standeth or falleth." Romans 14:4.

[21] See p. 12, above. Grotius regarded the regulation of religion as one of the principal aspects of public law. See pp. 99, 133, 172, below.

[22] The *Defense* likewise lacks the structural perfection and stylistic elegance which characterize the *Introduction* and the *Law of Prize*.

chief executive, Jefferson Davis,[23] have been of less interest to lawyers than the labors of a comparably eminent Confederate jurist, Judah P. Benjamin, in the field of private law.[24]

I.

Grotius begins the preface (dated June 7, 1622, at Paris) with a Dutch proverb: though lies move fast, truth catches up at last.[25] It is not strange, he explains, that his justification did not see the light until several years after the change of government in Holland, and his unjust condemnation. (Those events took place in 1618.) He was prevented from an earlier demonstration of his innocence by a number of factors: his confinement for nine months at The Hague, followed by his imprisonment at Loevestein under a stricter regime than the sentence called for. "Delivered from this imprisonment by God's merciful blessing I needed time to obtain what was required for the justification, not so much of myself (a mere servant) as of my masters (the States of Holland)."[26] He then outlines his

See p. 29, above, and p. 150, below. But see note 42, below, regarding the orderly sequence of treatment exhibited in the *Defense*.

[23] Jefferson Davis, *The Rise and Fall of the Confederate Government*.

[24] Judah P. Benjamin, *A Treatise on the Law of Sale of Personal Property*.

[25] *Defense*, iii [References will be to the Dutch edition of 1622 unless otherwise stated. Page numbers in the preface will be given in Roman numerals.] The proverb reads:

> Al is de Leughen snel,
> de Waarheydt achterhaaltse wel.

[26] *Defense*, iii–iv: "Van die ghevanghenisse door Godes ghenadigen zegen verlost zijnde, heb ick tijd van doen ghehadt om te becomen dat tot Justificatie, niet zoo zeer van my, die maar een Dienaar ben gheweest, als van mijne Meesters, mij noodigh was." See also pp. 16, 87–88, above, and p. 93, below.

argument that the proceedings and sentence against him were void and contrary to law; that the judges were without jurisdiction and were not impartial; and that he was denied a trial before his own sovereign (the States of Holland) or a proper judicial tribunal. Moreover, had such transfer of the proceedings been permitted, it would have been fruitless because of an unconstitutional change of personnel in the public bodies of Holland effected through the *coup d'état* of 1618. Hence the only means of demonstrating his innocence to posterity and to dispassionate observers was to publish the *Defense*.[27]

Grotius then reviews briefly the religious disputes which led to his arrest. Although opponents of the Calvinist doctrines of unconditional predestination, limited atonement, irresistible grace, and perseverance of the saints had long been permitted to preach peaceably at Utrecht, Gouda, Hoorn, and other places, they were challenged by the Calvinists. The States of Holland, which under the Union of Utrecht retained sovereignty and had authority in the matter of church affairs, directed that these controversial topics "not be treated except in a sober and edifying manner" and that both sides "live together in brotherly love."[28]

But the Calvinists held separate, secret gatherings, and in some instances took possession of churches and expelled their opponents by force. They spoke disrespectfully of the authorities of Holland, and urged that a national synod be held. They won Prince Maurits to their side. He attended a Calvinist church of separatist views, and directed the army to disregard instructions of the government of Holland in connection with matters arising out of religious dis-

[27] *Defense*, iv. See also note 34, below.
[28] *Defense*, iv–v. On this admonition, see also *Defense*, 47, 55.

putes. Holland, on the other hand, vigorously contended that no national synod could be convened without its consent, and that the army was bound to respect the sovereignty of Holland in the matter of religion, to enforce its decrees with regard thereto, and support its magistrates in putting down breaches of the peace when disorder arose. As there were suspicions regarding the loyalty and dependability of some of the troops (especially after the orders of Prince Maurits mentioned above), and as some cities had no garrisons, their local militia were called into service to keep order. Under long-established rules of law the cities and States of Holland had the unquestioned right to maintain such forces.[29]

The States of Holland protested against certain attempts of the judicial courts to interfere with measures adopted by the States. They also protested against calling a national synod by the States-General. This gathering (the Synod of Dort) was comprised for the most part of theologians favorable to the Calvinist cause; and those of differing beliefs were condemned, expelled from their churches, and compelled to go into exile.[30]

[29] *Defense*, vi–vii. For further details, see *Defense*, 105, 220, 235. At Rotterdam a company had been in service for twenty or thirty years. Grotius saw its flag on the city hall. *Defense*, 117, 225. Sovereignty includes the use of arms to maintain internal order (common defense was entrusted to the States-General). *Defense*, 106.

[30] *Defense*, viii, x. The Hooge Raad (as to which see note 46 below) had no appellate jurisdiction in "matters of state," including measures of forced removal of suspected persons (like the Nisei in California during World War II). Likewise there was no appeal permitted in cases under "extraordinary" or summary procedure (as to which see *Defense*, 158, 163, 216, 224). The States of Holland decided whether a case was of this type, the Hooge Raad meanwhile staying proceedings. The Hooge Raad (unlike a court under American constitutional law) had no power to disobey acts of the States

Prince Maurits went to Utrecht and demanded that the militia disband. Grotius and other delegates of the States of Holland were there, under instructions to assist the States of Utrecht and to warn the regular troops not to disregard the orders of the States of Utrecht in matters reserved to the respective provinces and not committed to the authority of the States-General. However, the local militia were disbanded, for the sake of peace and in the hope of effecting an accommodation through the efforts of France, which sent a special ambassador to the Netherlands for the purpose of promoting a settlement of the religious disputes.[31]

But as soon as the militia had been dispersed, eight persons, acting as the States-General, ordered the arrest of Grotius, Johan van Oldenbarnevelt, and Rombout Hoogerbeets. The States of Holland and the cities under whom they held office protested this action. In spite of the prisoners' objections that the States-General had no jurisdiction, that body set up a special political tribunal, which proceeded to condemn them.[32]

Besides numerous procedural irregularities, Grotius complained of the falsehoods recited in the sentence. It asserted that Grotius had confessed to matters about which he had no knowledge and about which he had never been interrogated, much less been given a hearing and permitted to make a defense. "This and more would clearly appear if

---

of Holland. *Defense,* 128–31. Notwithstanding these long-established rules of practice, Calvinists complained of denial of justice when they resorted to the courts of judicature instead of the customary recourse to the States of Holland in connection with several instances of forced removal and cases under "extraordinary" procedure. *Defense,* 135.

[31] *Defense,* viii–ix. See also *Defense,* 249, 278–80.

[32] *Defense,* ix.

all I said on examination on every point were honestly made public without holding anything back or changing anything." Grotius demanded that a complete and unexpurgated version of his testimony be published.[33]

Grotius confidently asserted that the policy of tolerance and religious accommodation favored by Holland would have been more beneficial to the public than the policy adopted of unlawfully deposing public officials, expelling non-Calvinist clergy—to the sorrow of many pious Christians, and unjustly arresting and condemning him and his two associates.[34]

He repeatedly emphasized that nothing which he had done had been done on his own motion, but everything had been done by virtue of resolutions of the States of Holland or of the rulers of Rotterdam. To both of these authorities, and not to the States-General, was Grotius bound by oath of office. He had violated no allegiance but had accorded due respect to all lawful authorities, supreme or subordinate. Any complaint about his actions as a public servant should have been made to or against the masters he served.[35] Even if he had done anything in his individual capacity, he should not have been judged by his adversaries or

[33] *Defense,* x. See also *Defense,* 143, 159, 163.

[34] *Defense,* x–xi, 179, 296. See also *Defense,* 96–102, as to the ousting of officials. Prince Maurits conceded that this was contrary to the laws, and was not to be considered as a precedent. Grotius speaks with emotion of the fact that many of the deposed magistrates had served during the war at sieges of Haarlem, Leyden, and Alkmaar. *Defense,* 103.

[35] *Defense,* xi. "Indien yemandt over 't gunt by my als Dienaar was ghedaan hem wilde beclaghen, die most sijn actie niet jeghens my, maar jeghens mijne Heeren ende Meesters institueren." See text at notes 20 and 26, above. See also *Defense,* 136, 142, 152, 177, 180, 202, 215, 216, 217, 227, 247, 254, 263, 266.

by special judges or by anyone commissioned by the States-General; he should have been tried before the ordinary competent tribunals recognized by the long-standing provisions guaranteed in the Privileges of the Lands and cities. In defense of these rights, arms had been taken up against Spanish rulers in times past.[36]

Grotius then emphasizes the uprightness of his conduct, and refers to his reputation and past public services. "As to my intentions, I declare before God and the world, they were not other than to preserve the lawful government under which I was born and reared, and to bring the churches to unity, through reasonable accommodation not conflicting with God's word. . . . Those who judge otherwise of my intentions do me wrong without cause."[37]

Satisfied with his salary and good name, Grotius sought no additional prizes from the nation. In view, however, of his deserts, it would not have been without precedent if he had. "But what have I received as reward?" he angrily exclaims; nine months in prison without being permitted to see wife or children or friends although he was ill, condemnation as a criminal without fair trial, confiscation of his honorably acquired property, the circulation of false reports detrimental to his honor and good name, the persecution of his relatives, as if they were traitors. "Against all this my trust in God stands firm, who has delivered me so

[36] *Defense*, xii. As to the similarity of grievances of Grotius with those suffered by the Netherlands under Spanish rule, see also *Defense*, 135, 143, 155, 159, 162, 283, 285. As to "Privileges" granted by the feudal rulers as a source of law, see p. 133, below.

[37] *Defense*, xii. Besides his career as officeholder, Grotius refers to his zeal for Dutch honor and reputation shown in his published works and others unpublished but shown to some persons. This is a reference to his treatises on the history of Holland and the law of

miraculously, in good spirits and after the example of many pious servants of their country who have had to suffer, not because of their wickedness, but because of their virtue."[38] Indignantly denying the insinuations of an anonymous book[39] that he was sympathetic to Spain, he declared that he would obey the laws of France where he was living "with the intention of also doing service to my own country if I can."[40]

With a prayer for the unity of the nation, he assured his former adversaries that nothing he had said was said to injure anyone, but only as a necessary part of his defense. Much important and illuminating material had been omitted because it would have affected several distinguished persons. "But if I am pressed further," Grotius concludes threateningly, "I shall not be able to avoid speaking more pointedly and, without respect for the mighty, uncovering all secrets."[41]

II.

In the body of his book, Grotius first presents his justification of the States of Holland for the course pursued, in strict accordance with Dutch constitutional law, with regard to the religious controversies between Calvinists and Arminians (chapters I–XII). Then he treats at length and in logical order the defects of the procedure leading up

prize. See also *Defense*, 136, 214, 284, and pp. 29–30, 51–54, 77, above.

[38] *Defense*, xiii. See also *Defense*, 214, 246, 286.

[39] This was published in Latin at Venice by Josephus Bonafadius. Rogge, 97.

[40] *Defense*, xiv. See also *Defense*, 136, 170–72.

[41] *Defense*, xv. The concluding sentence is omitted in the Latin version.

to his condemnation (chapters XIII–XVIII).[42] Next follows the longest chapter in the book (chapter XIX), which contains a detailed annotation or commentary on every phrase of the sentence pronounced against Grotius by the special tribunal. The concluding chapter (chapter XX) discusses the extent of Grotius' acquaintance with the other victims of the prosecution by the States-General.

In the first part of the *Defense*, Grotius' principal thesis is that in the United Netherlands as confederated under the Union of Utrecht of 1579, sovereign power is vested in the individual provinces, not in the central government whose principal organ is the assembly known as the States-General. It is not surprising, Grotius says, that foreigners might suppose the States-General to be sovereign, since that body receives ambassadors and handles correspondence with foreign states.[43] Much historical evidence is marshaled by Grotius to demonstrate the accuracy of his analysis. For example, before the Union of Utrecht entrusting common defense to the States-General, Holland, and Holland and Zeeland, had fought wars on their own account. Article 1 of the Union of Utrecht expressly preserved the "Privileges, Freedoms, Rights, Statutes, praiseworthy Customs" of every province and city; these would include the province's prerogative of sovereignty.[44] The oaths of public officials

---

[42] These "nullities and excesses" are treated in successive chapters with regard first to those connected with his arrest; then those after arrest and before commissioning the judges; in the commissioning of the judges; after the commissioning but before the sentence; in the sentence; and after the sentence.

[43] *Defense*, 2, 145. Similarly Polybius remarks that for the same reason Greeks thought the Senate in Rome was sovereign, though the supreme power was really lodged *penes populum*.

[44] *Defense*, 4, 6.

prescribe allegiance to the States of Holland, and do not mention the States-General.[45] The Provinces have the powers of legislation and the administration of justice. Their laws are not submitted to the States-General for approval, but the States-General refer their laws to the provinces. There is no common court of judicature over the United Provinces. Coinage and public domain are in the hands of the provinces.[46] Linguistic usage points to the same conclusion. The name *"Gheunieerde Landen"* (United Provinces) shows that the provinces are separate states united; in the negotiations with Spain for independence the victorious Dutch were recognized as "free Lands, Provinces, and States. Now it is obvious that by freedom sovereignty is understood."[47] It would be unthinkable that Holland, having more than half of the wealth and population of the whole Union, would have surrendered its sovereignty to a body in which it would have no greater vote than the smallest of provinces, some of which had been liberated from Spanish rule and brought into the Union only through the sacrifice of Holland's blood and treasure (*bloedt ende goedt*).[48]

[45] *Defense*, 8. As to the dual oath of soldiers and of Prince Maurits as Governor General of Holland, see *Defense*, 118, 123, 221, 246, 258.

[46] *Defense*, 8–9. Holland and Zeeland established a joint appellate court (Hooge Raad), but the court of last resort in other provinces is entirely domestic. As to the powers of the Hooge Raad, see *Defense*, 128–34. (chapter xii).

[47] *Defense*, 9: "[V]rye Landen, Provincien ende Staten. Nu is kennelijck, dat met de vryheydt verstaan werdt Souverainiteyt."

[48] *Defense*, 12–13. Union on such terms would be as improbable as a marriage between a rich and a poor spouse on terms of community of property instead of in accordance with a prenuptial contract. In this analogy, as well as elsewhere in the *Defense*, Grotius shows his mastery of private law as well as constitutional and public law. See n. 140, below.

97

In matters of politics, experience is the best teacher, Grotius observes. Nature cannot be forced. The Netherlands has never, up to now, been successfully governed as a single state, though Alba and other Spanish rulers attempted to do so. Those who think it would be better if there were but a single state should in any event achieve their purpose openly, and not by usurpation and by oppression of God-fearing, patriotic citizens who obey the laws of and hold offices under the time-honored *de jure* governments under which they were born and reared.[49]

Innovators should also remember that often the evils of change are greater than those that flow from keeping something which is less perfect but already existing.[50] There are those who believe that it would be desirable if the whole world, especially Christendom, were governed by a single authority, but such proposals seem laughably impracticable. Similarly, it would be desirable if the whole world were united in a single religion. But in human life you cannot always get the best. Government must be conducted, not in accordance with someone's ideas as to what would be best and most advantageous, but in accordance with the public laws.[51]

The opinions held by Grotius are not of a sort "to disrupt the Union, but to maintain it scrupulously." Those that violate the Union are "those that do not comply with the terms of the Union, among which the chief is to maintain the Provinces in their rights, of which the most important is their sovereign government over the affairs of

[49] *Defense*, 11–12, 284. See p. 94, above.

[50] Compare the similar conservative views of Thomas Jefferson. Dumbauld, *The Declaration of Independence and What It Means Today*, 80–83.

[51] *Defense*, 26.

98

the Provinces. The Union was not formed in order to fuse these rights into one, but to maintain the same intact more effectively through mutual assistance. The old-time Hollanders had a saying: 'to each his own is the best way to keep peace; unfair dealing breaks friendship.' "[52]

From the possession of sovereignty by Holland, it follows that regulation of religion is accordingly a matter for the provincial authorities and not for the States-General.[53] In line with previous practice, Article 13 of the Union of Utrecht, the *sedes materiae* in Dutch constitutional law, expressly provided:

And touching the point of religion, the people of Holland and Zeeland shall settle it according to their discretion. And the other provinces shall have power to regulate theirs according to the content of the religious peace already drafted, or to order it therein generally or particularly as they shall find expedient for the peace and welfare of the provinces and cities and individuals thereof, and for the conservation of all spiritual and worldly goods and rights, without hindrance on the part of other provinces; provided that each individual shall remain free in his religion, and that no one on account of religion, shall be subjected to arrest or inquisition, following the Pacification of Ghent.[54]

[52] *Defense*, 13. See also *Defense*, 252, 281, 284. The proverb reads in the Latin version: "Hollandi veteres dicere solebant cuique suum ad pacis tutelam esse optimum: & iniquo commercio amicitias dissolvi." *Apologeticus*, 22.

[53] *Defense*, 14: ". . . bewesen zynde de Souverainiteyt van de respective Provincien, is ook met eene bewesen, dat de selve toecomt de dispositie over de Religie . . ." See also *Defense*, 85.

[54] *Defense*, 15. The Dutch text reads: "Ende aangaande 't Poinct van de Religie, sullen haar die van Hollandt ende Zeelandt draghen na haar-luyden goedt-duncken: Ende de andere Provincien sullen

The autonomy of each Province in matters of religion is shown by the declaration in 1579 that Roman Catholic provinces might join the Union. Was it likely that Holland would itself give up a freedom which it was willing to accord to such provinces? Nor was it possible, since the Union was a confederation where all members were on an equal footing, to interpret Article 13 as merely authorizing Roman Catholic provinces to change their religion by becoming Reformed, but not authorizing other provinces to regulate religion as they saw fit.[55] Grotius cites instances where individual provinces had established church regulations on their own initiative, and where Prince Maurits and the States-General had recognized the existence of such exclusive power in the provinces. Proposals to amend Article 13 so as to guarantee that all provinces should remain Reformed, unless a change was assented to by all provinces, had never been accepted; and such proposals were evidence that under existing law each province could act independently with respect to religion.[56] The legal situation created by the terms of the Union of Utrecht was not modified by the circumstance that later all the members of the confederacy were in fact adherents of the Reformed religion. This uniformity

hun moghen reguleren na het in-houdt van de Religionsvrede, alreede gheconcipieert, ofte daar inne generalijck, ofte particulierlijck alsulcke ordre stellen, als sy tot ruste, ende wel-varen van de Provincien, ende Steden, ende particuliere Leden van dien, ende conservatie van een yeghelijck, gheestelijck ende wereltlijck, zijn goedt ende gherechtig-heydt dienstelijck vinden sullen, sonder dat haar by de andere Provincien belet sal moghen ghedaan worden: midts dat een yeder particulier in zijn Religie vry sal moghen blijven, ende datmen niemandt ter cause van de Religie sal mogen achter-halen ende ondersoecken, volghende de Pacificatie van Gent."

[55] *Defense*, 15, 19–20.
[56] *Defense*, 16–17, 19, 24.

created no legal obligation. German principalities and Great Britain had also accepted the Reformed faith; but would it be said they were not free to change without the approval of the States-General, or of the Swiss of like belief?[57]

Grotius vigorously rejects the assertion that religion is the basis of the Union. He quotes a declaration of the States of Holland in 1576: "We have never taken up arms about religion." The Union, it is well known, was an outgrowth of the war against Spanish misrule, "the taking up of arms for freedom." The reasons for the war are reviewed on the basis of numerous documents covering the period of 1568–1594. Grotius concludes: "The real cause why arms were taken up was to preserve, against the innovating Spanish domination, a free Dutch government in accordance with the old laws, customs, and privileges, including freedom of conscience, under which without doubt is particularly embraced the freedom of the Reformed religion."[58]

He attacks the religious pretensions of his adversaries, saying that their lives and conduct show that real religion, "that is, the fear of God and the duty of a Christian man," does not touch their hearts. It is a great disservice to the public welfare to cause those citizens who are not adherents of the official religion to lose interest in the preservation of the state. It is not true that differences of religion harm the state. On the contrary, the state is injured when citizens are persecuted because of their opinions.[59]

The policy of tolerance and conciliation followed by Holland, Grotius contends, was permissible and practicable. Where questions of religious truth or scientific knowledge are concerned, the desire for certainty, for definite regu-

[57] *Defense*, 21. See p. 39, above.
[58] *Defense*, 3, 24–25.   [59] *Defense*, 36, 89, 229.

lation and final decision, which some churchmen sought and which would be suitable in settling lawsuits about property rights, is impracticable. Not every difference of opinion as to doctrine justifies schism in fellowship. Numerous divergences of view were tolerated in the early church, and in the Roman Catholic era over three hundred questions of doctrine were debated without schism. Even among the believers in absolute predestination themselves, there were divisions of opinion which did not cause separation; and disputes of greater importance, regarding the sacraments, had not led to disunion.[60] Since Calvinists fraternize with Lutherans and Anglicans, it is clear their attitude towards their Arminian fellow countrymen is a matter of faction, not of conscience.

Since advocates of a national synod desired it as a means for "decision" of disputed points rather than for discussion or accommodation, Grotius never believed it could do any good. It was not possible for a supporter of the lawful government of Holland to favor convoking a body whose revolutionary consequences were readily discernible. Yet Holland was willing to consent to a synod, if it could be conducted in a conciliatory and impartial fashion.[61]

---

[60] *Defense*, 35–38, 43, 45, 89. Compare the distaste for constitutional law, which he considered as not law at all but politics, which was felt by John Chipman Gray, that unrivaled master of property law. Dumbauld, "Judicial Review and Popular Sovereignty," *loc. cit.*, 197, 208. Calvin himself taught, as did Grotius, that diversity of opinion respecting nonessentials should not cause schisms in the fellowship of the church. Hugh T. Kerr, Jr., *A Compend of the Institutes of the Christian Religion by John Calvin*, 157 (IV, i, 12).

[61] *Defense*, 50, 54, 61, 71, 208. A national synod could not lawfully be convoked without Holland's consent. In 1597 Utrecht had vetoed a proposal for calling a synod. *Defense*, 17, 49, 196.

III.

Having demonstrated the lawfulness of his actions as agent of the government of Holland, Grotius goes on to show the procedural irregularities involved in his arrest and condemnation.

First, the arrest was vitiated by a fourfold illegality with respect to: (1) the parties making the arrest; (2) the parties arrested; (3) the place; and (4) the manner of arrest.

There having been no authorization by the States-General before the arrest, it was simply the action of private individuals. If it had been authorized by the States-General, it would have been an infraction of the Articles of Union and unlawful invasion of the sovereignty of Holland.[62] Moreover, the persons arrested were all members of the States of Holland and clothed with parliamentary privilege exempting them from arrest without the consent of the States of Holland. Furthermore, the Binnenhof, the place where the arrest was made, had long been a peculiarly sacrosanct public edifice within the territory of Holland. The States-General in occupying quarters there, along with the government of Holland, was itself enjoying the hospitality of Holland. Lastly, the arrest had been procured by fraud and deception. Grotius, while in the course of his employment in transacting Holland's public business, had been falsely informed that Prince Maurits wished to see him. No information having been made, the arrest was also in-

---

[62] *Defense*, 137, 139. On the day of the arrest, protests were made by the States of Holland, as well as by the city governments of Amsterdam and Leyden. Retroactive validity cannot be conferred, says Grotius, by later ratification (*"advoy"*) after deposing by force the lawful magistrates who had protested. *Defense*, 138, 140, 150.

curably void, under rules of criminal law dating from remonstrances against the practices of the Spanish Inquisition.[63]

The second charge levied by Grotius against the proceedings under which he had been condemned was that he had been denied a speedy trial. He had been confined for nine months without being permitted to see wife, children, friends, or counsel, although he had been suffering from illness during his detention. This treatment was a palpable violation of a Privilege dating from 1346 when Empress Margaret was Countess of Holland. The usual time permitted was six weeks, and the maximum (in time of war) was twelve weeks.[64]

Grotius complained that his examination had not been conducted in the presence of a judge, and had been interrupted by boisterous examiners who (like the judges later appointed) were themselves interested parties in the controversy. Not a word was said in the presence of the judges about many matters recited in the sentence, and with respect to approximately 10 per cent of the topics treated therein he had never been interrogated at all. More than once he was threatened with torture, which "is itself a kind of torture."[65]

The next criticism related to the composition of the tribunal before which he was tried. Grotius' twofold attack was directed both against the persons making the designation and against the persons designated to serve. The States-General had no sovereignty authorizing the exercise of judicial power over individuals. Article 17 of the Union of

[63] *Defense*, 141–42. Regarding the trial of Grotius, see Brandt, *Historie van de Rechtspleging* and Fruin, *Verhooren*.

[64] *Defense*, 142.

[65] *Defense*, 143, 145, 159, 161.

Utrecht recognized the jurisdiction of each province to administer "good law and justice" to its inhabitants as well as to foreigners. Moreover, since 1452 a Privilege *de non evocando* guaranteed the exclusive right of the local authorities to exercise judicial power. The States-General recognized the novelty and illegality of their procedure by expressly providing that it should not constitute a precedent. Similarly the judges demanded and received immunity before exercising their functions. It was Grotius' opinion that acts constituting so flagrant a violation of public law were absolutely null and void.[66]

Lack of impartiality was charged against the States-General and its appointees alike. The judges were later rewarded by political preferment. They were unlearned in the law and lacking in judicial experience. Why was not this case submitted to the *Hooge Raad* or to the provincial court of Holland, in accordance with the previous custom of the States-General, Grotius asked. It is odious, he said, in a free government to entrust the life, honor, and property of citizens to other than the ordinary judges, especially to persons who are political characters with no judicial training. This grievance was one of the evil practices of Alba which had led to the Dutch revolt against Spain.[67]

Irregularities occurring after the designation of the judges and before sentence was pronounced are next dealt with by Grotius. The first abuse discussed was the adoption of "extraordinary procedure." That form of summary proceeding should be used only where upon establishment of the facts the legal consequences would be clear. It was therefore

[66] *Defense*, 145–51, 154–55. "Tam notae leges ad ius publicum pertinentes efficiunt, vt nullum sit quod contra fit." *Apologeticus*, 271.

[67] *Defense*, 155.

entirely inappropriate in connection with a case such as Grotius', involving important controverted questions of law. Even where it is used, however, the defendant must be afforded an opportunity to consult counsel and present his defense. This includes the right to examine the information, call witnesses, and offer proof. Grotius was deprived of these privileges. He was denied the use of paper and ink, denied opportunity to dictate a statement, or to hear read what had been said previously. With his memory weakened by confinement and sickness, this was a denial of due process, as was the refusal to permit him to establish facts material to his defense. It was contrary to law for the tribunal neither to grant nor deny his demand to prove such facts, and then to assert in the sentence as established facts the contrary of what Grotius had asked leave to prove. Even the Spanish Inquisition always permitted the accused to consult counsel and to prove a defense. In the trial of Egmont, which was severely criticized in the Netherlands because he was denied counsel and witnesses, he was nevertheless permitted to present a written defense which is still preserved in the archives. After quoting the comments of Prince William the Silent of Orange on Egmont's case, Grotius apostrophizes: "Sir Prince, if you saw this that is now done, what would you say?"[68]

Grotius also complained that the scaffold was permitted to remain standing for several days after the execution of Oldenbarnevelt, while friends were sent to urge Grotius to seek pardon and promise silence, so as to make it appear that the prosecution had had some justifiable basis. But

[68] *Defense*, 158–59, 161. As to extraordinary procedure, see also Dumbauld, *Interim Measures of Protection in International Controversies*, 22, 44, 56–57.

Grotius and Hoogerbeets and their stouthearted spouses preferred suffering to dishonor. "God be praised for it, without whose mighty help we could not have resisted so many and such great temptations."[69]

Coming to the sentence itself, Grotius criticizes the inclusion in it of statements not based upon testimony. He also objects to the use, in unqualified form, of admissions made with qualifications. Another vital defect was the imposition upon Grotius and Hoogerbeets of the penalty of life imprisonment, that being a punishment not permissible under Dutch law.[70]

Dealing with irregularities after sentence, Grotius points out that the nature of the offense for which the accused had been condemned was not stated until the rendition of a supplemental judgment over a year later characterizing the crime as *laesa majestas*. Such an amendment could not be validly incorporated in a sentence, certainly not without first according the parties a hearing. In any event, the judges were not all present when the subsequent judgment was rendered.[71]

Grotius also viewed as grievances the seizure of his papers without inventory and the attempted confiscation of his

[69] *Defense*, 162–63.

[70] *Defense*, 163–65. In "extraordinary" procedure it is questionable whether a sentence may be based upon facts not confessed. Grotius' sentence asserted as facts not only things he denied, but things about which he had never been interrogated at all, much less permitted to make his defense and offer proof. *Ibid.*

[71] See p. 13, above; *Defense*, 167–68. The modification was made in order to confiscate property which otherwise would have gone to the family of Oldenbarnevelt. For recent cases regarding the necessity of all members of the court being present, see Ayrshire Collieries Corp. v. United States, 331 U.S. 132 (1947); Com. ex rel. Maurer v. Burns, 365 Pa. 596, 76 A.2d 383 (1950).

wife's property in defiance of a privilege enjoyed by him as a resident (*poorter*) of Rotterdam.[72] He also complained that the keeper of the prison was unduly severe in the restrictions imposed regarding the purchase of food and the freedom of Grotius' wife to come and go. The public was forbidden to speak to the family or servants or make any salutations of respect. But scandalous songs were permitted outside his windows. Later, after Grotius escaped through the efforts of his resourceful wife, the government attempted to spread false reports about him in France. But "God, who knows how innocent I am, will grant me good patience in this and all future sufferings." Notwithstanding all calumniations, Grotius was graciously received by the King of France and his ministers. The harsh treatment of Grotius by the Dutch will not diminish his abiding love of his native country "for whose freedom, peace, and welfare I shall always pray to God almighty."[73]

IV.

After having shown that everything done by him, for which he had been condemned, had been done by authority of the States of Holland or of the city of Rotterdam, and that those for whom he acted had not exceeded their powers

[72] *Defense*, 166. Not until after conclusion of a lengthy litigation in 1630 did Grotius' wife recover this property. The suit was still pending when the *Defense* was written. Philip C. Molhuysen, "De Bibliotheek van Hugo de Groot in 1618," *Mededeelingen der Nederlandsche Akademie van Wetenschappen, Afdeeling Letterkunde*, nieuwe reeks, Vol. VI, No. 3 (1943), 45; E. J. J. van der Heijden, "De Boekerij van Grotius," *Grotiana*, Vol. III (1930), 18, 21; G. Moll, "De confiscatie der goederen van Hugo de Groot," *Oud-Holland*, Vol. XX (1902), 83, 99, 107-12.

[73] *Defense*, 167, 169-72

as defined by Dutch public law, Grotius proceeds to comment in detail on the sentence pronounced against him by the tribunal.[74] This discussion comprises chapter XIX of the *Defense*.

Taking up the opening words of the sentence which merely identify the defendant, Grotius declares that he is not ashamed of his name. He states that he has borne it to the honor of his family and fatherland. But the judges were ashamed to sign their names to the sentence.[75]

After his name, his title is given: "former Pensionary of Rotterdam." Grotius specified other offices held by him, and also asserts that instead of being "former" pensionary he is still incumbent of that office, under the new government, as his appointment was under a contract not permitting him to be deposed.[76] (He later collected his arrears of salary.) This insistence upon his official status is not just vanity on the part of Grotius; it corroborates his contention that the conduct for which he was condemned was simply official business lawfully transacted on behalf of public authorities who were not subjected to the prosecution and punishment suffered by Grotius. That the servant should be treated as a criminal, while the masters retain their honorable status, irked Grotius and offended his keen sense of justice and propriety.[77]

"At present prisoner" were the next words of the sentence. Taken prisoner, says Grotius, by those who had no

[74] *Defense,* 173.

[75] *Defense,* 173. As to Grotius' aristocratic ancestry, see *Defense,* 212–13, where he is arguing that he would have nothing to gain by a revolution. As to his education, character, and habits of life, see also *Defense,* 284, 295.

[76] *Defense,* 174.

[77] See pp. 88, 89, 93, above.

lawful power to arrest him, and whose actions infringed the Privileges and legal rights of Holland. He refers to the previous discussion in chapter XIII on this subject.[78]

"Having confessed and it appears to the judges" evokes a reference to chapters XVI and XVII. Grotius resented being misquoted and being made to appear guilty of unlawful or unpatriotic conduct. He repeated his wish to have his testimony published in full, feeling confident that it would corroborate the statements in the *Defense*. "That I do not say anything herein beyond the truth will appear before all the world, if I can ever get my entire confession brought to light."[79] He declared that if he were guilty of the evil intent attributed to him in the sentence, he would have deserved death. Why was not that penalty imposed? Because he was actually innocent and the States-General, having unlawfully arrested him and imprisoned him for nine months incommunicado, wanted to make it appear to the public that he was guilty of some heinous offense.[80]

These examples illustrate the type of commentary which Grotius elaborates in this chapter, giving references to previous chapters in which he has discussed the matters raised by the passages of the sentence to which he directs his attention. As Grotius' method of treatment involves considerable repetition, only those comments that have particular interest will be mentioned here.

A glimpse of conditions of life in Grotius' time is given by his defense against the charge that he presented a protest from the States of Holland to the States-General "in an

[78] *Defense*, 175. For the discussion in chapter XIII, see p. 103, above.

[79] *Defense*, 175. See pp. 92–93, above.

[80] *Defense*, 278, 285. See also *Defense*, 162, 166, and 106, above.

irregular manner." Instead of being placed on the table of
the assembly, it was presented while the members were
not in their seats. They were trying to keep warm. Grotius
denies any irregularity. The instructions of delegates do
not limit them to the table, the whole chamber is at their
disposition, "and in the winter it is the custom of the
gentlemen to take counsel standing by the fireplace."[81]

Another charge was that the States of Holland had returned unopened to the States-General the letters calling a
national synod. Grotius defends this practice as customary
when a public body exceeds its authority.[82] In any event,
it is unjust to consider as criminal on the part of Grotius
and one or two other members an action which was taken
by the assembly as a whole.

It was also charged that Grotius had written documents
stating that the States-General had usurped the name of
the States-General in summoning a national synod. His
accusers had here fallen into absurdity in their effort to
show offensive behavior disrespectful towards the States-
General. It would be self-contradiction to say, and Grotius
had never said, that the States-General had assumed without authority the name of the States-General. But it was
correct to say, as he had said, that several provinces had
undertaken, without legal power, to act *ultra vires* in the
name of the States-General. If Gelderland, Zeeland, Vries-
land, and Groningen wished to call a synod in their own
name, they were free to do so; but they could not do so,

81 *Defense,* 201.

82 *Defense,* 202. The practice is sometimes employed even against
a body of higher dignity than the recipient. A fortiori the sovereign
States of Holland might properly resort to it.

lawfully, on behalf of the States-General, lacking unanimous consent of the provinces.[83]

Another revealing glance at customs of the time occurs when Grotius avers that he never got a penny from foreign governments, and never accepted anything from fellow Dutchmen except where it was such a trifle that it would have been discourteous to refuse. Similarly, Grotius explained that Oldenbarnevelt never took gifts except publicly, as the other envoys did when the Truce with Spain was negotiated, and that no law forbade such conduct, and that others received more than he did.[84]

Grotius stresses the unfairness of the charge that city magistrates were claiming sovereign power. They were merely acting under express authorization from the States of Holland, in attempting to maintain order.[85] There was no attempt to usurp power belonging to the States-General or to the Prince. Indeed, the militia called out by the cities would have been cheerfully placed under the command of the Prince to repel the attacks of foreign foes, if there had been any occasion to do so.[86]

---

[83] *Defense*, 206. See also *Defense*, 270. At another place Grotius points out an example of poor syntax as evidence of the unseemly haste with which his sentence was written: "Dit is quaat Duytsch . . . ." *Defense*, 275.

[84] *Defense*, 214, 246, 286, 289, 294.

[85] Grotius resents vigorously the description of the States of Holland "with great injustice" in the sentence as a "faction" and as his "accomplices." *Defense*, 235, 266. This resembles the reference to the House of Lords and the House of Commons in the Declaration of Independence as "others" with whom the King had combined in passing Acts of Parliament. Dumbauld, *The Declaration of Independence and What It Means Today*, 120.

[86] *Defense*, 226. Of possible interest to defendants in antitrust cases is Grotius' argument that he did not seek to "exclude" the

That neither the States-General nor the Prince had authority to act in contravention of the commands of the States of Holland (or of the States of Utrecht or any other province), in matters of internal police regulation within the province, was Grotius' definite and well-founded opinion.[87] He recognized that if the lawful authority of the province were challenged by force, it would be necessary to take up arms in defense of the law, as had been done of old against the King of Spain, or else to submit to the aggression to prevent bloodshed.[88]

Grotius did not believe that Prince Maurits would unlawfully use force to disperse the local militia without the consent of the provinces.[89] It would be contrary to law to bring soldiers inside the city gates without their first having taken the oath to obey the magistrates of the city.[90] Upon hearing that Prince Maurits would open the gates of Utrecht in defiance of the magistrates of the city, Grotius made the statement that "if I were in armed service and bound by oath to the States of Utrecht that I would rather witness such a thing than do it." He was not positive whether on that occasion he used the word "force" or not, "but

States-General or the Prince from any lawful authority. They cannot be "excluded" from exercise of an authority they do not rightfully possess. *Defense,* 225.

[87] *Defense,* 234, 257–58, 274.

[88] *Defense,* 246. The latter contingency ultimately occurred. The decision to yield in order "to avoid extremities" was advised by Grotius. "How are we now rewarded for this conciliatory attitude?" he inquired bitterly. He denied the charge of having endangered the person of the Prince. *Defense,* 279–80.

[89] *Defense,* 272–73.

[90] *Defense,* 127, 247, 258, 295. The soldiers were already bound to the province by their dual oath. See p. 97, above.

this I know well, that real Hollanders are no courtiers and are accustomed to give everything its right name."[91]

That his opinions would result in disruption of the Union or create an *imperium in imperio* Grotius stoutly denied. On the contrary, he declared that he was maintaining and preserving the established form of government. "All nations like to be governed according to their old customs," he observed. "In all my writings I have defended the sovereignty and freedom of the land."[92]

After further declarations of patriotism and prayers for divine protection of the nation,[93] Grotius concludes his commentary on the sentence by referring to the formalities of its rendition: the place was one where his masters were sovereign; the time was nine months after his arrest and fifty-one years to the day since the sentence against Egmont; and the judges were men who would not sign their names.[94]

V.

Grotius' acquaintance with other victims of the Calvinist purge forms the subject of the final portion of the *Defense* (chapter XX).

First and foremost is Oldenbarnevelt. "That he had any inclination to serve the Spaniards or their adherents I have never perceived in his actions or words," Grotius declares. Some of the elder statesman's divergences from what Gro-

[91] *Defense*, 277.

[92] *Defense*, 280–81, 284. See pp. 98–99, above.

[93] *Defense*, 284–86. Grotius compares his innocence and suffering with that of Joseph in the Bible. *Defense*, 285. This theme was later elaborated in his play *Sophompaneas* (1635). *Schets*, 104.

[94] *Defense*, 286. See note 75, above.

tius would have preferred took on a sinister interpretation when it was assumed, as his captors falsely told Grotius in prison, that it was certain that Oldenbarnevelt had been corruptly dealing with Spain. Grotius later became convinced that these charges were pure invention put forth for the purpose of making Grotius lose courage. This became evident when nothing was said in Oldenbarnevelt's sentence about such treason.[95] That Oldenbarnevelt's intention had been "to surrender the sovereignty of the Provinces to any foreign power I have never been able to observe or to believe." Though Grotius was a young man at the time of the Armistice negotiations with Spain and did not meddle in what was not his business, he concluded that of the two opinions prevailing with respect to continuance or cessation of hostilities, Oldenbarnevelt chose the more humane and favorable to life. This opinion was shared by the Kings of France and England. Oldenbarnevelt favored alliance with those two powers as the best support of Dutch freedom.[96]

Of Johan de Haan, pensionary of Haarlem, Grotius says that his sentence did not fit the offense of which he was condemned. Grotius first made his acquaintance in the States of Holland.[97]

"It grieves me when I come to Hoogerbeets," Grotius continues. This pious and courageous man had been a dear friend of Grotius in freedom; and although in the Castle of Loevestein they were not permitted to see each other, their friendship was continued by means of correspondence.

[95] *Defense,* 288.
[96] *Defense,* 290.
[97] *Defense,* 292–93.

Hoogerbeets had served twenty years on the *Hooge Raad*, "an example of a perfect judge."[98]

In speaking of Johan Uitenbogaert, Grotius recalls being placed by his parents, when a youth, in the home of Franciscus Junius at Leyden and in that of Uitenbogaert at The Hague. This association with the pious and learned preacher was a beneficial experience for which Grotius never ceased to be grateful. He always went to hear Uitenbogaert preach whenever he had the opportunity, and admired his great gifts of wisdom and eloquence. As to the offense with which Uitenbogaert had been charged, concerning a meeting held at his house where Grotius, Hoogerbeets, and de Haan conferred with the Secretary of the States of Utrecht regarding dismissal of the militia, Grotius observes that Uitenbogaert was not present during the entire discussion, and that when he was there he never said a word.[99]

In conclusion, Grotius notes that he did not become acquainted with Daniel Tressel, a former clerk of the States-General, until their exile brought them together. While Tressel was not found guilty of *laesa majestas*, Grotius was at a loss to know why he had been accused and tried at all. It was general knowledge at the time, that he had often talked with Oldenbarnevelt and other deputies in the States-General, without any criticism by anyone. Grotius states of his own knowledge that when a meeting between

[98] *Defense*, 293–95. Grotius points out that the acts of the city government of Leyden for which Hoogerbeets was condemned had occurred before he took office as pensionary of that city (a post he held only for eight months).

[99] *Defense*, 295. See also *Historie*, I, 122.

the representatives of Holland and of Utrecht was held at Tressel's house, Tressel was not present.[100]

The *Defense* ends with a fervent prayer: "Now having completed what I owed to my conscience, to my wife and children, and to others for the information of the present and of future generations, I pray to the merciful God that He will graciously pardon all those who have sinned against me or others; and protect my dear native land against all internal and external attacks; and grant to Prince Maurits that he may govern the land happily and with the affection and gratitude of the good inhabitants; and make fruitful in men's hearts the teachings that tend towards piety; and strengthen me and also others who suffer for the same cause with His spirit, in order that we may not only bear patiently the cross with which He honors us, but may thereby better our life more and more, and so finally being redeemed by His infinite mercy out of this vale of tears we may participate in the glory which our Lord and Savior has gained for us."[101]

VI.

To the modern reader, the *Defense* is perhaps more significant for its treatment of the relation of church and state than for its discussion of Dutch constitutional law and criminal procedure. Grotius was thoroughly Erastian in his views, believing that the sovereign had paramount authority in religious matters.[102] Religion being regarded

[100] *Defense,* 296.
[101] *Defense,* 296–97; *Apologeticus,* 533.
[102] See p. 15, above.

as a political question, it was perhaps only natural that Grotius (like the French *politiques*) should favor a policy of accommodation, compromise, and expediency, seeking to bring about conciliation among the various sects rather than the domination of any particular creed.[103] This position was directly contrary to the clerical or Hildebrandine[104] concept (held by both Roman Catholic and Calvinist adherents) which viewed the church as supreme over the "secular arm" or political government. A third view, strict separation of church and state, was not widely held until proclaimed by Thomas Jefferson in the Virginia Statute for religious freedom and incorporated in the First Amendment to the Constitution of the United States. This doctrine is perhaps peculiarly American, although it can find Scriptural support in the injunction to render unto Caesar the things that are Caesar's, and unto God the things that are God's.[105]

Grotius' position was similar to that of the Church of England in its middle-of-the-road position.[106] Not only was the Anglican church in its origin a religion created by Act of Parliament,[107] but subsequent developments, quite in keeping with English habits, expressed an attitude which

103 *Defense*, 28–30.

104 So named for Hildebrand, who as Pope Gregory VII compelled Emperor Henry VI to make homage at Canossa, barefooted in the snow. Bryce, *The Holy Roman Empire*, 158–60.

105 Mark 12:17; Luke 20:25.

106 See p. 11, above.

107 The Act of Supremacy, 26 Henry VIII c. 1 (1534). After the American Revolution, another Act of Parliament authorized English bishops to ordain Americans. Before passage of this Act it was thought that perhaps it would be necessary to resort to Danish bishops to propagate the Anglican faith in America. *Works of John Adams*, VIII, 349.

was superficial and illogical, but workable. Professor Gilbert Murray refers, as an illustration, to

. . . the religious teaching established in state schools by the Act of 1870. There were two or three possible views which might claim to be logical. If Parliament knew what religious doctrine was true, it should have that doctrine taught in the schools. . . . If Parliament did not know what religion was true, it could either abstain from religious teaching altogether . . . or it could allow all sects . . . to inculcate their particular preferences. Parliament did none of these things. It accepted a motion from a private member, Mr. Cowper Temple, authorizing the teaching of Christianity, but ordaining that "no religious catechism or religious formulary distinctive of any particular denomination shall be taught in the schools." Disraeli . . . riddled the clause with hostile criticism. It was unintelligible; it founded, on the spur of the moment, a new religion; it made the teachers into a new sacerdotal class. Yet, as a matter of fact, the clause expressed the real fundamental wish of the best minds of the nineteenth century, it stood the test of experience, it enabled religious teaching to move as men's aspirations moved, and it did in a rough-and-ready way separate the kernel of religion from the husk of dogmatic theology. Established religions do not cut a very distinguished figure in the history of human thought, but that unconsciously created by Mr. Cowper Temple is perhaps, for practical purposes, about the best there has ever been.[108]

[108] Gilbert Murray, *The Ordeal of This Generation*, 47–48. Compare Thomas Jefferson's belief that "the interests of society require the observation of those precepts only in which all religions agree." Dumbauld, "Some Modern Misunderstandings of Grotius," in *Volkenrechtelijke Opstellen ter ere van de hoogleraren B. M. Telders*, 66. An effort to devise a prayer of that sort for use in New York schools

The attitude of Grotius was likewise practicable and expedient. But it is important to note that Grotius did not favor tolerance as an end in itself, merely because it was politically advantageous. He did not consider all religions as equally true or false; he did not hold that it was immaterial or unimportant whether a religion was true or false; he did not treat truth and falsehood as equivalent from the standpoint of the welfare of the state. He viewed tolerance as a means of testing competing faiths in order to determine truth.[109] It was permitted only with respect to details not essential to salvation. Grotius did not go beyond advocacy of "accommodation not in conflict with God's word."[110]

Grotius recognized the inefficacy of attempts to solve religious conflicts by geographical separation of the disputants or by insistence upon politeness and forbearance in the conduct of their controversies. For it would be foolish to try to prevent disputants from demonstrating the absurdities

---

was stricken down by the Supreme Court in Engel v. Vitale, 370 U. S. 421, 422, 424, 430 (1962).

[109] Free inquiry and debate were regarded by Thomas Jefferson as the only effective means of "sifting out the truth either in religion, law, or politics." Jefferson to George Washington, September 9, 1792, *Works of Thomas Jefferson*, VII, 146. Similarly Justice Holmes said in Abrams v. United States, 250 U. S. 616, 630 (1919): "Persecution for the expression of opinions seems to me perfectly logical. . . . But when men have realized that time has upset many fighting faiths, they may come to believe even more than they believe the very foundations of their own conduct that the ultimate good desired is better reached by free trade in ideas—that the best test of truth is the power of the thought to get itself accepted in the competition of the market, and that truth is the only ground upon which their wishes safely can be carried out. That at any rate is the theory of our Constitution."

[110] *Defense*, xii, 37.

of their opponents' position. If that were forbidden, how could they gain converts to their own views?[111]

There is a lesson for the present age in these observations of Grotius. Too often, nowadays, one notes a tendency to believe that "all facts are created equal."[112] This results in the adoption of an attitude of tolerance which is basically nothing more than abdication of judgment[113] and acceptance of complete skepticism and indifferentism: one must treat all opinions with tolerance because the search for truth is an impossible or at least unimportant quest. In any event, a pliable expediency, avoiding anything that might offend any influential group, has become the touchstone of a mild-mannered culture which seeks to eschew the "controversial."[114]

Perhaps another useful lesson is taught by the history of the religious wars and crusades. They ended, not when one side gained victory over the other,[115] but when it was recognized by both sides that each was too strong to be defeated and that the effort to win was too costly.[116]

[111] *Defense*, 45.

[112] Zechariah Chafee, Jr., *The Inquiring Mind*, 25.

[113] Thus is is often said that all nations were equally guilty of causing World War I; but "such a view implies a complete abandonment of the duty of thinking and weighing evidence." Murray, *The Ordeal of This Generation*, 67.

[114] The insipid character of most moving pictures and much broadcasting is partly due to acceptance of the view rejected as absurd by Grotius which glorifies inoffensiveness.

[115] Jefferson, although advocating freedom of inquiry and debate, was doubtful whether anyone ever convinced an adversary by argument. Propagation of a religion or political party, he believed, was best accomplished by propagation of the species. Jefferson to J. T. Randolph, November 24, 1808, *Works of Thomas Jefferson*, XI, 81.

[116] Jefferson in his Notes on Virginia emphasizes that over the earth so many religions exist that any particular one is necessarily a minority, and others cannot be "gathered into the fold of truth"

May not the same reasons in due time bring about the cessation and atrophy of the ideological struggle[117] which now divides the world into two opposing camps, each of which apparently has the ability to annihilate the other, along with itself, in a universally destructive holocaust?

by force. "Reason and persuasion are the only practical instruments." *Works of Thomas Jefferson*, IV, 80.

[117] As to the essential nature of this struggle as a competition between salvation-religions for the allegiance of mankind, see Charles Lowry, *Communism and Christ*, 37, 39, 143, 159.

Introduction to the Jurisprudence of Holland
Inleidinge tot de Hollandsche Rechts-geleerdheid

The University of Leyden Press published in 1952 a handsome edition (undertaken at the initiative of E. M. Meijers, an eminent law professor in that ancient seat of learning) of one of the best-known works of Hugo Grotius.[1] Though less familiar to lawyers outside the Netherlands than the world-famous *De Jure Belli ac Pacis*,[2] or than the earlier (but long unpublished) work *De Jure Praedae*[3] in which as a young practicing lawyer Grotius developed the doctrines given currency in the book of 1625, the *Introduction to the Jurisprudence of Holland* has enjoyed in its author's native land an authority substantially equal to that of Blackstone in common-law countries.[4] It was the first com-

---

[1] *Inleidinge tot de Hollandsche Rechts-geleerdheid* [hereinafter cited as Dovring] (Dovring, Fischer, and Meijers, eds., 1952).

[2] Concerning the book 1625, see pp. 57–82, above.

[3] Concerning this work, see pp. 23–56, above.

[4] During the revisal of the laws of Virginia after the American Revolution had begun, Edmund Pendleton proposed to adopt Blackstone by statutory enactment, but the suggestion was rejected by the revisers in favor of a more modest program of law reform. *The Papers of Thomas Jefferson*, II, 314.

prehensive work on the substantive civil law of Holland.[5]
For more than a century and a half this systematic textbook served as the foundation for academic instruction in
civil law at Dutch universities, and from 1859 to 1901 it
had the force of law in South Africa in cases not covered
by code provisions.[6]

The most convenient edition for English readers will still
be that of R. W. Lee, who in 1936 published a commentary
intended to have practical value for lawyers in South African
courts.[7] An authoritative Grotius bibliography published in
1950 devoted thirty-four items to the *Introduction*.[8] Prior
to the present volume, the most recent Dutch version was
that of Fockema Andreae, as revised by L. J. van Apeldoorn
in 1939.[9]

[5] *Schets*, 80. It should be mentioned *in limine* that by "Holland"
is meant not the whole Netherlands, but the Province of Holland and
West Friesland, of which Grotius was a high official at the time of
his arrest in 1618.

[6] See *Bibliographie*, 350.

[7] *The Jurisprudence of Holland* [hereinafter cited as Lee] (Lee's
trans.). The first volume prints on opposite pages the Dutch text
and the English translation. (The text follows the second edition
of 1631, with Lee's emendations). The second volume contains the
editor's commentary. "It is intended, as the original work was intended, for students of law who are to be lawyers; and for lawyers,
who have retained from their studies the knowledge that an apt citation from Grotius may give weight or ornament to an argument.
Doubtless, this classical work may be approached from different
points of view. . . . But the writer . . . has been more concerned to
bring Grotius into relation with the law of to-day; to answer the
question which a practitioner might put to him, 'What use can I
make of Grotius in Court?' " Lee, I, v. Earlier English translations
were published by Charles Herbert in 1845 and by Andries A. F. S.
Maasdorp in 1878 (reissued 1888 and 1903).

[8] *Bibliographie*, 349–68. Item Nos. 757–90; the present edition,
then in preparation, was listed as No. 785.

[9] A prior edition of this appeared in 1926. Fockema Andreae's

The first edition of the *Inleidinge*[10] appeared in 1631 at The Hague, published by the widow van Hillebrant Jacobsz van Wou. A second edition by the same publisher was printed in the same year. This second edition of 1631 is used by the present editors, as well as by Lee and by Fockema Andreae and van Apeldoorn, as the basis of their text. The original manuscript was burned by Grotius while in prison lest it fall into unfriendly hands. Three unauthorized editions were issued in 1631, for as an exile Grotius was denied copyright in his work. During the lifetime of Grotius nine editions were published. From 1631 to 1939 there were twenty-eight editions, besides five English translations appearing from 1845 to 1926. A translation into Latin, which Grotius had desired, was prepared in 1835 but was not published until 1962.[11]

The present edition incorporates annotations and corrections made by Grotius in 1639 on the margin of a copy of the edition of 1636. This copy was brought to light at Lund, Sweden, in 1948 by Folke Dovring, one of the edi-

1910 edition omitted, as it had been reprinted in Fruin, *Verspreide Geschriften*, VIII, 10, the introductory essay by Robert Fruin on the history of the *Inleidinge* during the life of its author. This essay, entitled, "Geschiedenis der Inleidinge tot de Hollandsche Rechtsgeleerdheid gedurende het leven des auteurs" and found on pp. xv–xxxii of Vol. I, adds to the value of Fockema Andreae's first edition published in 1895.

[10] Interesting variations in the spelling of the title occur. The ornate, engraved title page says *Inleiding tot de Hollandsche Rechtsgeleertheyd*. The bastard title reads *Inleiding* but *Rechts-Geleertheid*. The caption on the first page reads *Inleidinge* and *Rechtsgeleerdheid*. Apparently Grotius' preference throughout the book was for this last-mentioned form of spelling, while the preface uses a still different variant *Rechtsgheleertheydt*. Fruin, *Verspreide Geschriften*, VIII, xxiii.

[11] Dovring, xi, xiii, xvi, xvii.

THE LIFE AND LEGAL WRITINGS OF HUGO GROTIUS

tors.[12] The transcription of this new matter was made by
Dovring at Lund from the original, and by Fischer at Leyden from a photographic reproduction. Their versions were
later compared. Notes by Dovring (translated, checked, and
supplemented by Fischer) are added.[13] The paragraph divisions first introduced in the edition of 1727 are preserved.
Typographical emphasis is supplied as desired by Grotius.
A third distinguishing feature of the present edition is its
effort to interpret Grotius by resorting to Grotius himself.[14]
Hence the annotations, instead of references to numerous
sources of old Dutch law, contain, as a rule, only parallel
passages and other relevant material from other writings of

[12] Folke Dovring, "Une partie de l'héritage littéraire de Grotius
retrouvée en Suède," *Mededeelingen der Koninklijken Nederlandsche
Akademie van Wetenschappen, Afdeeling Letterkunde*, nieuwe reeks,
Vol. XII, No. 3 (1949), 239, 248. The library of Grotius was sold
by his widow to Queen Christina of Sweden, whom Grotius served
as ambassador from 1634 to 1645. Edmund Griepenhelm and Isaac
Vossius, royal librarians, received part of their perquisites in the form
of duplicate volumes. The library of Griepenhelm was brought by King
Charles XI and given to the University of Lund in 1684. This explains
the presence there of the 1636 edition of the *Inleidinge*. Dovring was
also able to identify a number of other books as having belonged to
Grotius. The library of Vossius was bought by the University of Leyden in 1689. (*Ibid.*, 242–43.) Similar identification of Grotius' books
at Leyden was made by Professor E.M. Meijers. Meijers, "Boeken uit
de Bibliotheek van de Groot in de Universiteitsbibliotheek te Leiden,"
*Mededeelingen der Koninklijken Nederlandsche Akademie van Weten-
schappen, Afdeeling Letterkunde*, nieuwe reeks, Vol. XII, No. 3
(1949), 251-79. For other volumes see Folke Dovring, "Nouvelles
recherches sur la Bibliothèque de Grotius," *Mededeelingen der Koninklijken Nederlandsche Akademie van Wetenschappen, Afdeeling Letterkunde*, nieuwe reeks, Vol. XIV, No. 10 (1951), 331–38.

[13] Most of the variant readings in the text are the work of Dovring, while the references to other passages of the *Introduction* or
other writings of Grotius are the work of Fischer.

[14] Dovring, xii–xiv.

Grotius. These include, besides works such as *De Jure Belli ac Pacis*,[15] his published legal opinions and correspondence.[16]

Appended to the book are five synoptic charts prepared by Grotius himself showing the analytical divisions of the treatise, and a table showing degrees of relationship for inheritance.[17] An alphabetical index compiled by Grotius,[18] and an index of Latin and bastard-Dutch law terms with their equivalents in genuine-Dutch,[19] likewise from the hand of Grotius, are added.

In addition to the preface to the first edition (which purports to be written by the publisher, but was probably supplied by Grotius himself or in accordance with his suggestions by his brother Willem) the editors print a letter from Grotius to his three sons covering the same ground.[20]

Here Grotius states that he had not at first intended to publish the *Inleidinge,* but had prepared it for the instruction of his sons. Copies got into circulation, however, and by 1628 he was finally persuaded to permit its publication in order to prevent defective versions from being printed.

[15] Dovring, 395–99 (Appendix V), is an extract from Grotius' *History of the Goths* praising Germanic law as preferable to Roman because its precepts are "simple, short, and clear." See pp. 155–56, below.

[16] See Dovring, 350–94 (Appendix IV). Most of these opinions are available in English in de Bruyn, *The Opinions of Grotius as Contained in the Hollandsche Consultatien en Advijsen.* For a discussion of legal points found in Grotius' correspondence, see Christiaan Vaillant, *Disputatio Juridica Exhibens Interpretationem Locorum Quorumdam Juris in Hugonis Grotii Epistolis.*

[17] Dovring, 322–36 (Appendix I).

[18] Dovring, 337–39 (Appendix II).

[19] Dovring, 340–49 (Appendix III).

[20] Dovring, xxix–xxx (preface); *ibid.,* xxvii–xxviii (letter). Regarding publication of the book, see also Fruin, V*erspreide Geschriften,* VIII, xx–xxvii.

In the preface Grotius also explains that he has sought to treat everything in its proper order, taking as a model the Justinian *Institutes*.[21] He also emphasizes the importance of accurate terminology. He has taken care to see that his definitions correspond with the terms defined, a matter wherein many legal scholars have gone astray, and also to see that the various divisions of the topics treated follow in proper sequence. (His analytical plan is shown in the tables or charts attached.) From Roman law he has set forth "that which is in use amongst us" whether from the *Institutes* or other law books, and has added "our own law" insofar as known to him from old charters, judgments, and other sources.

Regarding language, Grotius says: "I have sought to honor our Dutch mother-tongue and to show that this science of law can very well be handled in that tongue." To that end he has used a number of words now somewhat unfamiliar but which are "good old Dutch words" found in ancient legal documents, and he has also contrived some compound words, the meaning of which can readily be grasped. For the convenience of those who are accustomed to Latin or bastard-Dutch legal terms, he had placed such terms in the margin (marked with L. or B. as the case may be) wherever the genuine-Dutch equivalent of such terms occurs in the text.

---

[21] It is scarcely necessary to state that the *Institutes* are an introductory treatise (modeled upon the earlier treatise of the jurist Gaius) forming part of the *Corpus Juris Civilis* promulgated by the Eastern emperor Justinian in 533 A.D. The *Digests* cover the same ground in great detail, citing the opinions of jurists on the topics treated. The *Code* contains statutory enactments of the emperor, later additions to which were called *Novellae*. *Blackstone's Commentaries*, I, *81.

One thing he laments: that when he was writing this book in prison he had to rely too much upon his memory:

> I had few books and other helps by me, and also had no association with other men, of whom I had need in order to discuss the customs and usages of Holland. Seek therefore, the acquaintance of experienced jurists in order to supply what may be lacking here.[22] Accept this meanwhile as an inheritance, for the other property you would have inherited from me has been taken away, most unjustly. Keep God always before your eyes, and know that justice is dear to Him.[23]

The preface concludes:

> Herewith farewell. Use our work with as good pleasure as we have undertaken it. Read attentively, judge justly, and love all those who hold Justice dear and seek to further the knowledge of law according to their ability.[24]

I.

Like *De Jure Belli ac Pacis*, the *Introduction to the Jurisprudence of Holland* is composed of three books. It is incomplete, however; there should have been four books, as

[22] Grotius thus recognized that forensic controversy and meeting of minds is an essential element in legal education. Sweatt v. Painter, 339 U. S. 629, 634 (1950).

[23] Dovring, xxviii. As to the language used by Grotius, see S. Vissering, "De rechts-taal van H. de Groot's Inleiding tot de Hollandsche Rechts-geleertheid," *Verslagen en Mededeelingen der Koninklijken Akademie van Wetenschappen, Afdeeling Letterkunde,* tweede reeks, Vol. XII (1883), 372–441.

[24] Dovring, xxx.

in the *Institutes* and Blackstone's *Commentaries*, dealing with the law of persons, things, obligations, and remedies, respectively.[25] Grotius never wrote the part about civil procedure.[26]

Chapter 1 of Book I treats of jurisprudence and justice. Jurisprudence is defined as the art of living in accordance with justice. Justice is a virtue of the will, impelling a person to do what is rightful. Rightful is what accords with right. Right, broadly speaking, is the harmony of the act of a reasonable creature with reason, insofar as another person is concerned with such act; narrowly speaking, it is the relationship existing between a reasonable creature and something that belongs to it, either by reason of dignity or of property. Dignity (*waerdigheit*) is the fitness of a reasonable creature for something that is desired. Property (*toebehooren*) consists of things (*beheering*) and obligations (*inschuld*).[27] The chapter concludes with a discussion of the Aristotelian categories of justice: universal and legal, distributive and commutative.

[25] In the *Institutes* the law of things spreads over into the first twelve chapters of Book III, while the law of obligations similarly continues through the first five chapters of Book IV.

[26] Dovring, 10, 331. See Dovring, 1.2.26 (first book, second chapter, twenty-sixth paragraph), 2.46.6, 3.49.5. In the first table (Appendix I) Grotius says: "This part is treated by Merula, and therefore omitted by us." The reference is to Paulus Merula, *Synopsis Praxeos Civilis, Maniere van Procederen in dese Provincien Hollandt, Zeelandt ende West-Vriesland, belangende civile zaken.* New editions appeared in 1619 just before Grotius wrote the *Introduction* and in 1631 when it was published. Grotius does not speak of the treatise on civil procedure which his fellow prisoner Hoogerbeets was writing at Loevestein while Grotius wrote the *Inleidinge,* and which was annexed to certain later editions of Grotius' book. Vissering, *"H. de Groot's Inleiding,"* *loc. cit.,* 386.

[27] See also p. 165, n.50, below.

Chapter 2 deals with the classification and operation of law. "The law [*lex*] (which is also sometimes called right [*jus*] because it prescribes what is right) is a work of reason, ordaining for the common good something that is honorable, established and proclaimed by someone who has authority over a community."[28]

A law can have three effects: (1) to create obligation; (2) to prescribe punishment for violation; and (3) to nullify acts conflicting with the law.[29]

Laws may be classified according to their source or according to their subject matter.[30] According to source, all law is natural or positive.[31] Natural law is the judgment of the understanding, making known what things are by their very nature honorable or dishonorable, with an obligation from God to follow such judgment.[32] Natural law is immutable.[33] Positive law is that which has its origin from the will of its establisher.[34] It is divine or human.[35] Since the coming of Christ we know no other divine positive law than that which God the Father has revealed to us through the same Christ our Lord.[36] Human positive law

[28] Dovring, 1.2.1 (italics removed), *Blackstone's Commentaries*, I, *44.

[29] Dovring, 1.2.2.

[30] Dovring, 1.2.3, 1.2.24.

[31] Dovring, 1.2.4.

[32] Dovring, 1.2.5. The definition of natural law, and indeed the entire analysis contained in this chapter of the *Inleidinge*, should be compared with that found in the *Law of War and Peace* and the *Law of Prize*. See pp. 37–40 and 62–64, above.

[33] Dovring, 1.2.6.

[34] Dovring, 1.2.7.

[35] Dovring, 1.2.8.

[36] Dovring, 1.2.9.

is the law of nations (*volcker-wet, jus gentium*) or the civil law (*burgerwet, jus civile*).[37]

The law of nations is that which is accepted by nations generally for maintaining the community of the human race.[38] This resembles somewhat the law of nature, and because of widespread and long-continued usage can be modified only with difficulty. The same is true of the law of ambassadors and many other things concerning peace and war.[39]

Civil law is that which has its origin in the will of the rulers of a civil society.[40] It may be peculiar to one people or common to several, but in any case may be changed by one nation without the consent of others.[41] Civil law is written or unwritten.[42] Written law in the province of Holland and West Friesland is either general throughout the province or peculiar to a locality.[43] General written law consists of resolutions of the states (that is the knights, nobles, and good cities) or of commands of the provincial rulers to whom, in the capacity of counts, lords, or otherwise, such power has been lawfully delegated by the states.[44] Local

[37] Dovring, 1.2.10.

[38] Dovring, 1.2.11. This doubtless refers to the "*societas humani generis*" spoken of in the *Law of Prize*, p. 55, n. 163, above.

[39] Dovring, 1.2.12. See pp. 38–40, above.

[40] Dovring, 1.2.13.

[41] Dovring, 1.2.14. See Dovring, 2.3.14 and p. 39, above.

[42] Dovring, 1.2.15.

[43] Dovring, 1.2.16.

[44] Dovring, 1.2.17. See Lee, I, 517, where it is said that the statement of Grotius is historically inaccurate: "In early times the Counts of Holland exercised legislative functions, which were not, as Grotius implies, derived from the States, but antedated the existence of the States as legislative authority." *Ibid.*, II, 2: "The power of the Counts, originally feudatories of the Empire, was antecedent to the existence of the States."

written law is made not only by resolutions of the states as applied to particular localities, and by the provincial rulers through privileges (*hand-vesten, privilegien*) and special charters (*keuren*), but also by the *stadhouder*, president, and other councillors of the Court of Holland, and moreover by other officials empowered to make laws of local application.[45] Unwritten laws may also be customs common to the whole province or peculiar to a particular locality.[46]

With respect to subject matter all law is public or private.[47] Public law is that relating to religion,[48] the conduct of peace and war, the sovereignty and boundaries of the country, the power and manner of making laws and granting privileges, the power of adjudicating and disposing of public property, the punishment of wrongdoers and the functions connected therewith.[49]

Private law is that relating to the rights of persons to things, or the means of defending and pursuing the same (*i.e.*, substantive civil law and the law of remedies [*actiones*] or civil procedure).[50]

As mentioned previously, Grotius never did complete his *Introduction* by writing the part treating civil procedure. Nor did he write the part on public law.[51] Though recog-

[45] Dovring, 1.2.18. See Lee, II, 2–3.
[46] Dovring, 1.2.21.
[47] Dovring, 1.2.25. See p. 172, below.
[48] See p. 11, above.
[49] Dovring, 1.2.26.
[50] Dovring, 1.2.28.
[51] Dovring, 331. See note 26, above. Proper treatment of the public law of Holland called for particular care, and he could not handle this topic adequately without access to his papers and those of others. Meanwhile, much of that field was covered by his *Apologeticus* and his *De Antiquitate*. See p. 149, below. In Appendix I (table I)

nizing that public law is more important and weighty than
private law, Grotius states that it will be better to treat
private law first, since it is more ancient than public law.
In the succeeding chapters of the *Introduction* he proceeds
to expound in comprehensive fashion the private law of
Holland.[52]

II.

Grotius commences his consideration of the law of persons with a chapter containing reflections on birth, marriage, family, government, political society, crime, and
slavery.[53] Descending from these philosophical views to
the specific provisions of the civil law of Holland, Grotius
distinguishes between persons *sui juris*, competent to man-
age their own affairs and litigate in their own name, and
those lacking such capacity. The incompetent, who are under the guardianship of another, have such status by reason of marriage, infancy, or unfitness.[54] The conditions and
consequences of marriage,[55] the tutelage of children whose

Grotius says: "The treatment hereof was postponed by us until a better opportunity [*tot beter gelegentheid*]. Meanwhile, a great part
of this can be understood from our published books." See Lee, II, 6.
It is unfortunate that Grotius never completed this task, as his service
in the office of *Advocaat-Fiscaal* brought him great familiarity with
criminal law and Dutch constitutional law. See *Schets*, 29, 37.

[52] Dovring, 1.2.27.

[53] Dovring, 1.3.–. Slavery is a punishment particularly used against
"those who, in the manner of beasts, had injured other men in body
and goods by force, that is by unjust war." Dovring, 1.3.8, 13. On
the familiar Grotian theme of just war, see pp. 34, 43, 66, above.

[54] Dovring, 1.4.3. Except for a few vestiges of feudalism, "all men
in these provinces are deemed to be free." Dovring, 1.4.2.

[55] Dovring, 1.5.–. With the growth of commerce in Holland a
married woman engaged in trade is free from her husband's tutelage

parents are living,[56] the appointment[57] and powers[58] of guardians for orphans, or for defective persons and wastrels,[59] are next treated. Grotius then deals with the status of legitimate and illegitimate issue,[60] of natives and aliens,[61] of nobles and commoners,[62] and of clergy and laity.[63]

III.

Book II, the lengthiest in the *Inleidinge*,[64] deals with the law of things. Before coming to the legal rights in and to things, it opens with a chapter defining and classifying

and may act for herself in all matters affecting the business. Dovring, 1.5.23. A husband's power over the wife's property may also be limited by antenuptial contract and by separation of goods. Dovring, 1.5.24.

[56] Dovring, 1.6.–. .

[57] Dovring, 1.7.–.

[58] Dovring, 1.8–10.–.

[59] Dovring, 1.11.–.

[60] Dovring, 1.12.–. The principal distinction remaining relates to the right to inherit. Dovring, 1.12.8. See also 2.15.7, 2.16.6, 2.27.28, 2.31.–, 2.41.29–30.

[61] Dovring, 1.13–. Commerce has rendered the distinction between natives and aliens relatively unimportant. Dovring, 1.13.3.

[62] Dovring, 1.14.–. The only remaining distinction is that nobles have the right of hunting hares and rabbits, and barons moreover may take one hart yearly. Dovring, 1.14.7. The distinction among those not noble, between "well-born" and "common people," has likewise lost significance. Dovring, 1.13.8–9.

[63] Dovring, 1.15.–. As, since acceptance of the reformed religion, all privileges of the clergy both in litigation and other civil-law rights have ceased, this distinction is of no importance except insofar as public law is concerned. Grotius never wrote the discussion of public law which he promised here and elsewhere, *e.g.*, Dovring, 1.11.10, 1.14.6, 2.1.29, 2.1.57, 3.32.6. See note 51, above. The four topics treated in this sentence of the text are instances of *qualitas*; what precedes is concerned with *relatio*. Dovring, 1.3.7, 1.11.9–10.

[64] In the present edition Book I contains 40 pages; Book II, 153; and Book III, 138.

things. A thing (res) is "whatever is external to man and in any way useful to man."[65] Things are classified, inter alia, as corporeal or incorporeal; movable or immovable; and as belonging to all mankind, to a great community, to individuals, or to no one.[66] In connection with individuals Grotius recognizes as "inalienable" a person's life, body, liberty, and honor—things that belong to one in such fashion that they could not belong to someone else.[67]

Grotius then divides the legal rights to things into two familiar categories: rights of property (jus in rem) and obligations (jus in personam). The first is a relationship between a person and the thing without regard to other persons. The second is a right that one person has against another to require from the latter some thing or act.[68]

Grotius then passes to the topics of possession[69] and ownership.[70] Ownership is complete or incomplete.[71] The

[65] Dovring, 2.1.3, Lee's translation. Lee, I, 65.

[66] Dovring, 2.1.9–10, 2.1.16. A discussion of the high seas, the Zuider Zee, navigable rivers, public buildings, cemeteries, and family foundations then follows. See Lee, II, 63.

[67] Dovring, 2.1.42. See Dumbauld, The Declaration of Independence and What It Means Today, 58–63, 69. But suicide is punished in Holland, Grotius goes on to say, and no one may dispose of life or body or freedom by contract (except in marriage). Moreover, freedom may be forfeited by crime. Dovring, 2.1.44-47.

[68] Dovring, 2.1.58–59.

[69] Possession is defined as the actual holding of a thing with intent to hold it for oneself and not for another. Dovring, 2.2.2.

[70] Ownership is such property in a thing that someone out of possession can obtain it by resort to law. Dovring, 2.3.1. Grotius devotes a lengthy passage to reconciling the legitimacy of individual ownership with his assertion that by the law of nature all things were in common. Dovring, 2.3.2. Grotius here states his frequently repeated notion of dominium eminens, that in civil society the law has greater power over persons and their rights and property than the persons themselves do. See also Dovring, 2.3.2, 2.5.2, 2.7.4,

modes of acquisition and loss of ownership are next discussed.[72] These include taking possession of things without an owner (as wild animals),[73] transfer of things from the previous owner,[74] prescription,[75] significant transformation in good faith of another's material,[76] or commingling of goods, accession, or alluvion.[77]

Acquisition of entire estates by marriage[78] or by succession by will[79] or intestacy are then treated in detail.[80] It should be noted that, in accordance with Roman law, a testament or "complete last will" is one which establishes a direct heir.[81] An heir is a person who steps into the place

3.1.21, 3.26.2. Compare Jefferson's view that property is a right derived from the state, not from the law of nature (hence "pursuit of happiness," rather than property, is mentioned in the Declaration of Independence). Dumbauld, *The Declaration of Independence and What It Means Today*, 61.

[71] Complete ownership is that which permits one to do with a thing anything he pleases that is to his advantage and not forbidden by law. Dovring, 2.3.10.

[72] Dovring, 2.3.12.

[73] Dovring, 2.4.–.

[74] Dovring, 2.5.–. Fruits or income from property is acquired by the person having bona fide possession. Dovring, 2.6.–.

[75] Dovring, 2.7.–.

[76] Dovring, 2.8.2–4. As painting upon another's canvas. Grotius believes the same results should follow from writing on another's paper, though the Roman law is otherwise. Reasonable compensation must be made to the former owner of the material.

[77] Dovring, 2.9–10.–.

[78] Dovring, 2.11–13.–.

[79] Dovring, 2.14.3. As to wills see *Blackstone's Commentaries*, II, *12–13.

[80] Dovring, 2.26–32.–. Who may make a will is treated in Dovring, 2.15.–; who may take, in 2.16.–; how a will is made, in 2.17.–; how a will fails to take effect, in 2.24.–.

[81] Dovring, 2.17.3. A will not doing so is known as "incomplete" or as a "codicil." As to codicils see 2.25.–. Institution of a direct heir is necessary to the "completeness" (*Volkomenheid*) of a will. (Lee

137

of the testator as universal successor, taking over both benefits and burdens, assets and liabilities.[82] A direct heir is one
whose rights come directly from the deceased; an indirect
heir (or heir at second hand) is one who is to receive the
inheritance from a direct heir.[83] Some persons not only
may, but must, be named as heirs for their "legitimate
portion." Thus children must be given at least one-third of
what they would have received in case of intestacy; if there
are more than four children they must receive one-half.[84]
However, this rule does not apply if the children are guilty
of certain undutiful acts.[85] Parents must be made heirs only
if they would have been heirs in case of intestacy, and have
not been guilty of improper conduct toward the decedent.[86]
Brothers and sisters may complain of disinheritance only
if an infamous person has been made heir.[87] Contrary to
Roman law, an heir subject to an impossible condition is
regarded as not an heir, and a person may be made heir
from or until a particular date.[88]

An heir may renounce the inheritance, or deliberate for a

---

translates as "validity." Lee, I, 151.) See Dovring, 2.24.6. If the
will contains a clause that if it cannot take effect as a "complete"
will it shall take effect as a codicil, the heir by intestacy must treat
the defectively instituted direct heir as an indirect heir and hold the
estate for his benefit. Dovring, 2.24.7. See Lee, II, 143.

[82] Dovring, 2.14.7. A person taking something under a will but
not as heir is a legatee. Dovring, 2.14.13. As to legacies see Dovring
2.22–23.–

[83] Dovring, 2.14.12. The status of an indirect heir is similar to
that of beneficiary of a trust or *fidei-commissum*. See Dovring,
2.20.–.

[84] Dovring, 2.18.5–8.
[85] Dovring, 2.18.13.
[86] Dovring, 2.18.15–16.
[87] Dovring, 2.18.17.
[88] Dovring, 2.18.20–21. See Lee, II, 154.

year whether to accept.[89] He may accept with benefit of
inventory under certain circumstances, and is then liable for
debts only to the amount of the assets of the estate.[90] A
direct heir who voluntarily accepts an inheritance may de-
duct from it a fourth part, and is then liable for debts to
the extent of his portion but not for legacies. This privilege
originated in Roman law under the Trebellian *senatus-con-
sultum*.[91] By the *lex Falcidia* the heir is entitled to abate
legacies to the extent necessary to leave him a fourth of his
inheritance after payment of debts and funeral expenses.[92]

Upon completion of his discussion of wills, Grotius takes
up intestacy. The first distinction to be made here is between feudal[93] and allodial property. With respect to the
latter, the next distinction is whether the decedent was
born in wedlock or not. In case of legitimacy, the inquiry
then is whether or not relatives survive sufficiently close
to inherit.[94] If so, the inheritance passes according to generally applicable law[95] or according to the law specially

[89] Dovring, 2.21.4.
[90] Dovring, 2.21.8.   [91] Dovring, 2.20.6.
[92] Dovring, 2.23.20. This rule does not apply if the will provides
otherwise, nor does it apply to charitable bequests or property left with
a prohibition of alienation. The heir may also lose his right by negli-
gent administration of the estate.
[93] Feudal property is treated in Dovring, 2.31–33.–, among other
types of property rights less than absolute ownership. See Dovring,
2.3.10–11; and p. 137, n. 71, above.
[94] Dovring, 2.27.6–9. The degrees of relationship (ascending,
descending, and collateral) are described in 2.27.–. Escheat occurs
only upon lack of relatives in the tenth degree, as computed by Roman
law. Dovring, 2.30.1. See Lee, II, 183. The degree of consanguinity
in Roman law is determined by counting up to the common ancestor
and then back down to the person whose degree of relationship is
to be ascertained. *Blackstone's Commentaries*, II, *207.
[95] The *lex loci rei sitae* is followed for immovables, the law of the
place where the succession opened for movables.

chosen to govern the particular inheritance in question.[96] The right to choose the system of law to be applied was unknown to Roman jurisprudence, and arose by reason of the great diversities of local law in Holland. Accordingly, in antenuptial agreements provisions were included to govern the succession to the property of children of the marriage. This choice of law took effect if the children died without issue and without having made a lawful will. The children could dispose of the property by will or *inter vivos*, but if they did not, the property passed according to the law chosen in the antenuptial agreements.[97] Parents might also in their will make the choice of law with respect to property left to their descendants. Choice of law can also be made in case of settlement or separation of goods made in the orphans' court for the benefit of minor children by parents contemplating remarriage.[98] A more generous settlement on the children is likely to be made if choice of law is permitted so as to provide that if the parent outlives the children the property will revert to the donor.

The two principal systems of local law were known as "*aesdoms-recht*" and "*schependoms-recht*." These terms were derived from the names of the local judicial officials in the respective regions where the two systems grew up. The old Dutch word "*doemen*" meant to render a judgment or "doom"; and the judgment of an "*azig*" was called "*azigdom*," which by abbreviation became "*aesdom*." The judgment of "*schepenen*" was called "*schependom*." Ac-

[96] Dovring, 2.27.10.

[97] Relatives of the wife might wish to prevent the husband from investing the wife's wealth in lands normally subject to a law which would permit her property to pass to him if he outlived wife and children.

[98] Dovring, 2.29.–. As to separation of goods, see Dovring, 1.9.6.

cordingly, *"aesdoms-recht"* was the law of North Holland, akin to that of West Friesland, while *"schependoms-recht"* was the law of South Holland, akin to that of Zeeland. The Ijssel River was the dividing line, broadly speaking, between the two regions. An attempt was made in 1580 to adopt a uniform law throughout the Province of Holland and West Friesland, principally following the *"schependoms-recht,"* but a great variety of local divergence nevertheless continued to prevail, and in different localities different combinations of the principal features of the two old systems were in force.

The chief principle of the Frisian law was that "the nearest blood takes the goods." No representation *per stirpes* was admitted; children of a deceased child took nothing if any child of the prior generation remained. If a child died before its mother, after inheriting from its father, the property passed to her. Half-brothers and full-brothers were treated alike. The fundamental rule of the Zeeland system, on the other hand, was that "the goods must go where they came from" (*materna maternis, paterna paternis*). Hence a parent outliving a child did not inherit. If both parents were dead, the property was divided into the "four quarters" (or eight-eighths if necessary), representing the various ancestral strains, and if one of them failed escheat occurred rather than inheritance by the other lines.[99]

Grotius concludes the topic of intestate succession by considering the case of persons without relatives close enough to inherit, and to persons born out of wedlock.[100] He briefly mentions how complete ownership is lost,[101] and then

[99] Dovring, 2.28.–.   [100] Dovring, 2.30–31.–.
[101] Dovring, 2.32.–. See Dovring, 2.3.12, and p. 137, above.

enters upon an analysis of the various types of incomplete ownership. These include servitudes,[102] use and enjoyment (*dominium utile*),[103] usufruct (use and enjoyment for life),[104] hereditary use and enjoyment (*emphyteusis*),[105] feudal tenure,[106] use and occupation (*usus*),[107] titheright,[108] ground rent[109] and superficies (the right to a building on someone else's ground),[110] ownership in expectancy,[111] and security interests (*onderzetting*).[112]

This completes the treatment of rights *in rem* contained in Book II.

IV.

In Book III Grotius turns to the topic of obligations (or

[102] Dovring, 2.33.–37.–. See Lee, II, 186, 196.

[103] Dovring, 2.38.–. This is the right to all the fruits of a thing but without diminution of the thing itself,.

[104] Dovring, 2.39.–.

[105] Dovring, 2.40.–.

[106] Dovring, 2.41–43.–.

[107] Dovring, 2.44.–. This is the right to enjoy advantage from a thing, but not all the fruits or profits. It generally continues during the life of the grantee.

[108] Dovring, 2.45.–. Curiously enough, this means the right to take one-eleventh of the fruits.

[109] Dovring, 2.46.2.

[110] Dovring, 2.46.8.

[111] Dovring, 2.47.–. This right seems similar to that of the beneficiary of a shifting or springing use.

[112] Dovring, 2.48.–. This term is not exactly the equivalent of a mortgage, pledge, or lien as understood in Anglo-American law. The interest may be created by operation of law, as well as by express act. Dovring, 2.48.7–21. It may be general, covering all the pledgor's property, and this binds movable property, but does not bind the property in the hands of a purchaser for value (*titulo oneroso*). A later special pledge of particular immovable property takes priority over an earlier general pledge.

rights *in personam*). His analysis of this branch of the law, like all such descriptions of this phase of the Roman-law system, will seem strange to lawyers familiar only with the Anglo-American common-law system. Contracts and torts, which in common-law thinking seem to lie at opposite poles of the juristic horizon, are both treated by the Roman-law jurists as aspects of the law of obligations, to wit, obligations *ex contractu* and *ex delicto* respectively. Besides uniting what is dissimilar, the Roman system subdivides the simple concept of contract into a variety of separate types of transactions. To those who are trained to consider a contract as a promise (or set of promises) to which the law attaches binding obligation, it seems superfluous to distinguish contracts made by utterance of a particular formula (*spondeo*), contracts by entries in the parties' books of account, and those dealing with particular types of situations (sale, hiring of services, hiring of work to be done, etc.). Nevertheless, certain phenomena in the legal system with which we are familiar may help us to grasp the notions of the Roman lawyers: contracts under seal or containing a statement in accordance with the Uniform Written Obligations Act[113] "that the signer intends to be legally bound" are surely as good examples of formalism as the Roman *spondeo*; and insurance policies with their standard clauses[114] are surely as appropriate an illustration of a peculiar type of contract for meeting the needs of a particular situation as anything to be found in Roman law.

Grotius begins with a general discussion of obligations, finding in natural law a twofold source from which they

[113] Pa. Stat. tit. 33, §6 (1936).
[114] Pa. Stat. Ann. tit. 40 §§510, 510.1, 510a, 511 (Supp. 1951).

arise: contract and inequality.[115] But the provisions of civil law govern the matter.[116] Rules as to capacity to incur obligation and authority to obligate other persons are then treated,[117] as well as impossible or prohibited contracts.[118]

Coming to the various particular types of contracts, he discusses in turn donation,[119] suretyship,[120] compromise (a contract between litigants for disposing of a lawsuit),[121] obligations in writing,[122] and agreements (*contractus, overkoming, handeling*).[123]

Agreements, based on the dealings of the parties, are subdivided into numerous varieties. These are summarized by Grotius as follows:

5. Dealings are said to be without compensation when they consist in the giving of ownership, complete or incomplete. This is called gift or donation, and, if it is effected by last will, legacy. We have spoken of both of these already. If the dealing consists in giving the temporary use of a thing it is called loan for use; if in doing something it is called mandate; unless what is done consists merely in taking a thing into one's custody, when it is termed deposit: but, if the thing is taken by a creditor as security for a debt, it is called pledge or pawn.

[115] Dovring, 3.1.9.. Inequality covers something done for or given to another at his request without intent to make a gift, and also wrongdoing from which another suffers. Dovring, 3.1.17–18.

[116] Dovring, 3.1.21–22.

[117] Dovring, 3.1.25–38. See *Institutes*, 3.28.–.

[118] Dovring, 3.1.42–43.

[119] Dovring, 3.2.–.

[120] Dovring, 3.3.–.

[121] Dovring, 3.4.–.

[122] Dovring, 3.5.–. These are of three kinds: acknowledged before officials, before a notary, or bearing the obligor's signature.

[123] Dovring, 3.6.–.

6. With compensation: when the dealing consists in giving in order to receive in return; if complete ownership is given and a thing is transferred with the expectation of receiving a thing in return; then, if what is given admits of being measured, counted or weighed, and it is stipulated that a thing of the same kind shall be restored after a specified time, the contract is called loan for consumption: if one thing is given and some other thing is to be received in return it is barter: if money is given for ready money it is exchange: if a thing is given for money it is purchase and sale. If the dealing consists in giving incomplete ownership, then, if an hereditary lease is given on one side and money on the other, it is called hereditary lease or emphyteusis: otherwise it has no specific name: if the dealing consists in giving the use of a thing, then if money is to be given in return, it is termed letting and hiring: otherwise it has no specific name.

7. Other cases in which the dealing is with compensation are the following: if it consists in doing and something is to be done in return, then, if the contract relates to some business in which the parties are both interested it is called partnership; marriage may be brought under this head: in other cases it has no special name.

8. Again, a dealing may be with compensation in the sense that something is done on one side, and something given on the other: then, if what is given is money, the contract is called letting and hiring, just as when money is given for the use of a thing; but if what is done consists in taking upon oneself another person's risk, the contract is called assurance: if the compensation for what is done consists in something other than money, and what is done takes the form of an hereditary duty of homage, military service, or other service, then the contract is termed a feudal grant: otherwise it has no special name.[124]

[124] Dovring, 3.6.5–8, as translated in Lee, I, 335, 337.

Grotius follows closely the analysis found in his model, Justinian's *Institutes*. According to the Roman law there were four modes of entering into contractual obligation: by delivering of a thing, by words, by writings, or by consent.[125]

In the *Inleidinge* Grotius recognizes each of these categories. He also distinguishes between express contracts and those arising by operation of law or the dealings of the parties.[126] Express contracts are those entered into by words or by writings.[127] Those entered into by words required, under Roman law, the use of the solemn formula *spondeo* by the party to be bound.[128] Grotius says that on account of Dutch regard for good faith[129] the law of Holland does not follow these subtle formalisms of Roman law.[130]

With respect to contracts arising from delivery of property Grotius makes the same classification as Roman law: deposit (*bewaer-geving, depositum*) or bailment; pledge (*pand-geving, pignus*), the delivery of property for securing a debt; loan for use (*bruick-leening, commodatum*); and loan for consumption (*verbruick-leening, mutuum*), where

[125] Of obligations it is said in the *Institutes*: "Aut enim ex contractu sunt aut quasi ex contractu aut ex maleficio aut quasi ex maleficio." As to contracts: "Harum aeque quattuor species sunt: aut enim re contrahuntur aut verbis aut litteris aut consensu." *Institutes*, 1.13.2.

[126] Dovring, 3.1.49. See Lee, II, 270.

[127] Dovring, 3.1.50. Contracts by writing were discussed by Grotius in 3.5.–. See note 122, above. This type of contract in Roman law was accomplished by entries of "*expensa*" in the creditor's books of account at the debtor's direction. *Institutes*, 3.21.–.

[128] *Institutes*, 3.15.1.

[129] See pp. 7, 53, 72, above.

[130] Dovring, 3.1.51–52. Suretyship is treated by Grotius as a contract *verbis*. Dovring, 3.3.25.

an equivalent quantity of a commodity which can be weighed, measured, or counted is to be returned by the borrower.[131] In connection with the last-named variety of contract, Grotius is led into an extensive discussion on the propriety of interest and the evil effects of usury.[132]

As to contracts *ex consensu,* where no delivery of a thing is involved, Grotius expands the Roman-law classification by the addition of several species of agreement not mentioned in the *Institutes.* He enumerates mandate (*last-geving, mandatum*) or gratuitous agency; purchase and sale (*koop ende verkooping, emptio-venditio*); grant of an inheritable lease (*erfpachtgunning*); hire (*huir ende verhuiring, locatio-conductio*); partnership (*maetschap, societas*); insurance (*verzeeckering*); and feudal grant (*leengunning*).[133]

Grotius next treats quasi contracts, where obligation comes into existence by operation of law, without agree-

[131] Dovring, 3.7.1. Deposit is treated in 3.7.–.; pledge in 3.8.–; loan for use in 3.9.–; loan for consumption in 3.10.–. See *Institutes,* 3.14.–.

[132] Dovring, 3.10.8–10. Discussion of usury leads to mentioning bottomry, a type of loan where the risk of perils of the sea is assumed by the lender. Hence a higher rate of interest is permitted than on ordinary commercial loans. Dovring, 3.11.–.

[133] Dovring, 3.12.1. See *Institutes,* 3.22–26.–. Grotius deals with mandate in 3.12.– (bills of exchange, a special form of written mandate, are discussed in 3.13.–.); purchase and sale in 3.14–17.– (*naesting,* an interesting custom which permits relatives of the seller to take the place of the buyer, is discussed in 3.16.–.); grant of hereditary lease in 3.18.–; hire in 3.19.– (the importance of shipping to Holland leads to expansion of this type of contract as applied to shippers, skippers, and seamen in 3.20.–.); partnership in 3.21.– (here again contracts of mutual protection among ships and joint adventure among shipowners are separately treated in 3.22–23.–.); insurance in 3.24.–; and feudal grant in 3.25.–.

ment by the parties.[134] These obligations are shaped by analogy with the contracts of gift, mandate, or partnership.[135] Consideration is then given to unjust enrichment[136] and detriment. The latter is of two sorts. When someone gives or does something for another person upon request, and without the intent of doing so gratuitously, he would suffer detriment if not reasonably recompensed.[137] The other type of detriment is the injury inflicted by a wrongdoer.[138] Such conduct gives rise to obligation *ex maleficio* or *quasi ex maleficio*.[139] Corresponding to the types of rights previously described,[140] the types of wrongs recognized by the law may be classified as injuries to life, body, liberty, honor, and property.[141] In this connection Grotius emphasizes that crimes (as distinguished from torts) are created by positive law, not natural law, since a specific punishment must be prescribed, and this requires an act of legislative volition.[142]

The concluding portion of Book III consists of a discussion of the modes by which obligations are discharged.[143] Discharge is effected either by extinction[144] of

[134] Dovring, 3.26.2. See *Institutes*, 3.27.–.

[135] They are developed by Grotius in Dovring, 3.26–29.–.

[136] Dovring, 3.30.–. See also Dovring, 3.1.9, 14–18.

[137] Dovring, 3.31.1–2. See Lee, II, 331.

[138] Dovring, 3.32.2.

[139] *Institutes*, 4.1.– (*ex delicto*); *Institutes*, 4.5.– (*quasi ex delicto*). The latter type of obligation corresponds roughly to the common-law concept of "liability without fault." *Institutes*, 3.38.–.

[140] See p. 136, above.   [141] Dovring, 3.33–37.–.

[142] Although Grotius recognizes that there is an obligation arising from the law of nature to suffer punishment. Dovring, 3.32.7. See p. 60, above.

[143] Dovring, 3.39.1. In Roman law this is "*solutio*," or "*quo modo obligatio tollitur*." *Institutes*, 3.29.–.

[144] Extinction results from performance or its equivalent, or from

the obligation, or by nullification[145] thereof through the
use of certain legal remedies or defenses.[146]

V.

When Grotius decided to publish the *Inleidinge* and
forwarded the manuscript to Holland to be printed, his
brother Willem wondered if it was complete. Grotius ans-
wered this inquiry by pointing out that he had ended the
book with discharge of obligations. For treatment of judicial
remedies, the reader was to be referred to the treatise by
Merula; for treatment of public law, to other published
works of Grotius.[147]

release by act of the obligee or by operation of law, or from destruction
of the subject matter. Dovring, 3.39.3–6. Equivalents of performance
are deposit in court, merger, or setoff (3.40.–). Release by the obligee
is treated in 3.41–45.–; by operation of law (prescription, or statute
of limitations) in 3.46.–; by destruction of subject matter in 3.47.–.

[145] Legal remedies rendering obligations inoperative rest upon intrinsic causes (such as coercion or fraud) or extrinsic causes (such
as res judicata, bankruptcy, or *laesio enormis*). Dovring, 3.48–52.–.

[146] Dovring, 3.39.2.

[147] Fruin, *Verspreide Geschriften*, VIII, xxi–xxii; see notes 26 and
51, above. Writing to his brother on Jan. 9, 1629, Grotius said: "Ego
enim librum absolvi in modis tollendarum obligationum quia re vera
is finis esse debet partis tertiae, quae est de obligationibus, contra quam
in Institutionibus Justinianeis factum est. Pars quarta esse debuit de
actionibus et judiciis, sed eam omisi, quia Merula eas . . . tracta-
verat, et satis habui ad eum lectorem remittere. Pars altera, quae est
de publico jure quam etiam Justinianus in Institutionibus, non nisi
unica parte de publicis judiciis attigit, huic operi non accessit; meretur
enim curam singularem, sed expediri nequit nisi aditum habeam ad
chartas meas et aliorum. Interim bona ejus pars peti potest ex libro de
Apologetico et Antiquitate." Dovring, 331. Concerning Grotius' library, see Molhuysen, "De Bibliotheek van Hugo de Groot," *loc. cit.*,
45–63. The list of thirty-three books Grotius' wife was permitted to
take to him at Loevestein included Merula, the *Corpus Juris Civilis*,

"A monument more durable than bronze and loftier than the Pyramids' majestic pile I now have reared" was the boast of the Roman poet who first captured Greek song in Latin rhythms.[148] Of Blackstone, too, it has been said that he it was who first taught jurisprudence to speak the language of the English gentry.[149] Similar glory is due Grotius, merely from the standpoint of national linguistic pride, even if his only accomplishment were that of having embodied Roman law in the Dutch tongue. He would have gained lasting renown had he done nothing more than write this first great systematic treatise on the law of Holland for the instruction of law students in his land. But because of the intrinsic excellence which characterizes this book, its superb analytical power and orderly sequence of treatment, its clarity and conciseness, the *Introduction to the Jurisprudence of Holland* merits the encomium of jurists. It deserves to rank with the author's earlier *Law of Prize* as a masterpiece of structural perfection.[150]

Rightful pride and patriotic sentiment impel Grotius to say of this widely used book, when speaking of his un-

works on feudal law, the law of the sea, and the law of antenuptial pacts, as well as writings of Cicero, Soto, Peckius, and Cowell, the English legal writer. *Ibid.*, 62–63.

[148] "*Exegi monumentum aere perennius*
   Regalique situ pyramidum altius . . .
   Dicar, qua violens obstrepit Aufidus . . .
   Princeps Aeolium carmen ad Italos
   Deduxisse modos." Horace, *Carmina*, III, xxx.

[149] D. Douglas, *The Biographical History of Sir William Blackstone*, 139, quoting Jeremy Bentham's preface to *A Fragment on Government*, xli–xlii.

[150] See page 29, above. The entire book is symmetrical, but these qualities may be particularly noted in the passages we have analyzed in some detail above, notably the classification of law in 1.2.–, and the modes of dissolving obligations in 3.39–52.–.

requited services to his country: "The trouble taken by me to make known to all our people their ancestral laws, for the honor and fame of Holland, well deserved, to my way of thinking, that a ship be sent to bring me home, as the Athenians in olden days did for Demosthenes for lesser service."[151]

[151] Grotius to his brother-in-law, Nicholas Van Reigersberg, Dec. 13, 1631: "Ik verwonder my zeer over de . . . groote bitterheit tegen my betoont. Na zoo lange gevankenisse, na verbeurtmaking mijner goederen, geduurende eene uitlandigheit van tien jaren, in't midden van veel ongelijx en hoons, aen my en alle de mijnen, heb ik alle gelegentheden gezocht om't Land en allerley ingezetenen van dien te dienen naar het vermogen dat by my noch overig was . . . De moiete by my genomen om al ons volk zijne vaderlyke Rechten bekent te maken tot eer en roem van Holland, dunkt my dat wel verdiende dat men my een schip had gezonden om t'huis te komen, gelijk die van Athenen eertijdts aen Demosthenes om minder dienst gedaen hebben." Brandt and van Cattenburgh, *Historie van het Leven des Heeren Huig de Groot*, I, 422.

Florum Sparsio Ad Jus Justinianeum

Among the legal writings of Grotius there is a volume on Roman law which has received little attention. This is the *Florum Sparsio ad Jus Justinianeum*, published in Paris in 1642. The title page reads:

HVGONIS

GROTII

FLORVM SPARSIO

Ad Ius

IVSTINIANEVM.

PARISIIS,

Apud Viduam GVLIELMI PELE', via Iacobea,

sub signo Crucis Aureae.

1642.

I.

Whether the academic study of Roman law was undertaken by Grotius during his three-year sojourn at the University of Leyden is unknown.[1] In any event he had

---

[1] See van Eysinga, "Quelques observations sur Grotius et le droit romain," *loc. cit.*, 18–28. If Grotius did take any courses in law,

doubtless mastered that subject when on May 5, 1598, the
University of Orleans conferred upon him the degree of doc-
tor of civil law in the presence of the Dutch diplomatic mission which Grotius, at the age of fifteen, had accompanied
to France.[2] Letters written in 1615 counseling his brother
Willem regarding the latter's studies evince familiarity
with Roman law.[3] In a volume of poems, *Poemata*, published in 1617, is included a versified version of a portion
of Justinian's *Institutes*.[4] His *Introduction to the Jurisprudence of Holland*[5] was avowedly modeled on Justinian's
Institutes.[6]

The same scheme is pursued in an important part of
The Law of War and Peace.[7] References to Roman law
also abound throughout this celebrated treatise.[8] However,
it is essential to recognize that what Grotius was expound-

they dealt almost exclusively with Roman law, for in the university
curriculum of that era law was practically synonymous with Roman
law. See also Knight, *The Life and Works of Hugo Grotius,* 38, which
concludes that Grotius must have studied law only one year.

[2] See p. 4, above.

[3] Grotii, *Epistolae quotquot reperiri potuerunt,* 751–55 [herein-
after cited as *Epistolae*].

[4] *Institutes,* II, 1, *De rerum divisione et acquirendo earum dominio.*

[5] *Schets,* 71.

[6] P. 128, above.

[7] See pp. 66–67, above. After establishing that just war is a remedy
to enforce a legal right, Grotius catalogues the repertory of substantive legal rights enjoyed by potential belligerents under the system
of law with which he is dealing. This catalogue substantially para-
allels familiar topics of Roman private law. Grotius, *The Law of War
and Peace,* Bk. II, chaps. 2–17. This part of the work is not an
adventitious excrescence, but an essential and original part of the
system presented by Grotius. *Framework,* 102–103.

[8] But Grotius more than once warned against considering Roman
law as identical with the general law of mankind which he was ex-
pounding. *Framework,* 12.

ing in the *Law of War and Peace* was a system of universal
law common to and binding upon all mankind.[9] It was
based upon a threefold foundation: natural law, the law
of nations (*jus gentium*), and volitional divine law.[10] While
frequently referring to Roman law (as well as the civil law
of other states) as evidence of particular rules of natural
law or of *jus gentium*, Grotius clearly distinguished these
systems of law, and preserved his characteristic independence of judgment in formulating his own system setting
forth the law of humanity.[11] Moreover, some parts of his
system are drawn from other sources and exhibit no parall-
elism with Roman private law.[12]

It is also noteworthy that while engaged as ambassador
of Sweden at Paris, Grotius made a comparison of Roman
law with the *leges Barbarorum*, to the advantage of
the latter.[13] The occasion for this study grew out of his
desire to demonstrate that Sweden had more ancient titles
to diplomatic precedence than other nations whose ambassadors were given more favorable treatment at the court
of Louis XIII than Grotius. Hence he sought to use history as a weapon of statecraft.

Having concluded that the Goths and Vandals had their
origin in Sweden, he prepared a Latin translation of passages from the historians Procopius and Agathias. To these
historical materials Grotius added the laws of the Ostro-

[9] See pp. 59–61, 72, above.

[10] See pp. 62–64, above.

[11] Van Eysinga, *Sparsa Collecta*, 378–79 [hereinafter cited as
Sparsa Collecta].

[12] For example, chapters 20 and 21 of Book II on punishment,
and chapters 18 and 19 on the right of embassy and of sepulture.
Sparsa Collecta, 380; *Framework*, 103; see p. 67, above.

[13] *Sparsa Collecta*, 375–76; *Schets*, 111–12.

goths, Visigoths, Vandals, and Langobards, being convinced "that the genius and character of peoples can be
discerned from their laws no less than from their history
or that of their eminent men."[14] Not until 1655, ten years
after the death of Grotius, was this volume published by
Elzevir at Amsterdam, with the title *Historia Gotthorum,
Vandalorum, & Langobardorum.*[15] Contrary to the author's design, the laws were omitted but the "Prolegomena"[16] or preface contained a significant passage where
Grotius compared the Roman system of law with that of
the peoples of northern Europe, and evinced his prefer-
ance for the latter.[17] According to Grotius:

I see in the Roman laws too great subtlety, extending
even to trifling details, variety, inconstancy, and finally
such a vast and confused mass of materials that no one,
no matter how good his memory, can avoid having to look
up the statutory language frequently. But philosophy
calls for law that is simple, brief, clear, like the com-

[14] "[I] ta persuasus, non minus ex Legibus, quam a rebus gestis
populorum, aut in populis eminentium, ingenia conspici." *Historia
Gotthorum, Vandalorum & Langobardorum,* 63 [hereinafter cited as
Historia Gotthorum]; Dovring, 395–99.

[15] Grotius had forwarded the manuscript of the *Prolegomena* to
this work in 1637 to his chief, the Swedish chancellor Axel Oxen-
stierna, who praised it highly. Brandt and van Cattenburgh, *Historie
van het Leven des Heeren Huig de Groot,* II, 78–79, 140–41; *Epistolae,* 334–35, 869.

[16] The *Prolegomena* was separately reprinted at Marburg in 1746
with the title *Hugonis Grotii de veteri jure Germanico et Suecico
commentariolum. Bibliographie,* 332–35.

[17] This passage from the *Prolegomena* is printed as Appendix V
in Dovring. It also appears, with a parallel Dutch translation, in *Anthologia Grotiana,* 188–89. For a French translation, with comments,
see S. J. Fockema-Andreae, "Une Étude de Droit comparé par Grotius," *Grotiana,* Vol. X (1947), 28–44.

mands of the father of a family. Also long-standing duration without any change of itself gives great authority. I rejoice that I find these good qualities in the laws of our Northern people.[18]

Grotius then pointed to the widespread adoption of Gothic laws as a badge of merit, mentioning that "England is even now governed by the laws of the Normans." But if such acceptance is not sufficient, and it is required "that reason contend with reason," Grotius proceeded to a comparison between the two systems with respect to the principal topics with which law deals.[19]

In the field of public law, he found that the exercise of legislative power at Rome by one man (the emperor) was characterized by fallibility and fluctuation. On the other hand, the well-digested laws enacted among the northern European nations by the prince in conjunction with representatives of the people have three advantages: nothing noxious to the public interest can lurk undetected in legislation scrutinized by so many eyes; what is approved by common consent is obeyed more readily; and innovations

[18] "Ego in Romanis legibus subtilitatem minima quaeque persequentem, varietatem, inconstantiam, video, tantam denique molem, et in mole perplexitatem, ut nemo tam felicis sit memoriae, cui non saepe eveniat in leges incursare. At philosophia legem vult esse simplicem, brevem, claram; qualia sunt patrumfamilias in familiam suam imperia. Tum vero nihil mutata duratio multum secum habet auctoritatis. Haec ego in Septentrionalium nostrorum legibus invenire me gaudeo." *Historia Gotthorum*, 63–64. See *Sparsa Collecta*, 376; Dovring, 395.

[19] "[Pe]rcurramus ad collationem instituendam summa capita circa quae versantur leges." *Historia Gotthorum*, 65; Dovring, 396. Complete comparison was not attempted. "Materia infinita est de qua agit lex." *Florum Sparsio*, 87.

are introduced only when there is a real need for change.[20]

With respect to private law Grotius reviewed the rules applicable to marriage, wardship, contracts, property, intestate succession, and protection of possession against violence. In many ways he found that the laws of the northern European nations were more conducive than those of Rome to the stability and sanctity of marriage. Remarking that the Emperor Justinian married an actress, Grotius contrasted the Gothic laws requiring equality of rank between spouses. He also cited with approbation the praise of Tacitus and other writers for the Germanic custom prohibiting dowry; by their virtue, not by their wealth, women won husbands.[21] The Germanic peoples likewise were stricter in observance of the obligation of contracts than the Romans, Grotius believed. Intestate succession, a topic particularly confusing under the rules of Roman law, was regulated with clearness and simplicity among the northern European nations.[22]

[20] "[B]ene expensae leges tria habebant commoda, quod nihil publice noxium latere poterat inter tot monitores, quod prom [p] to animo servabantur quae communis consensus sanxerat, quod eadem numquam aut non nisi summa causa urgente mutabantur." *Historia Gotthorum*, 65; Dovring, 396. Likewise, with respect to public office among the Goths in contrast to the Romans, "nothing was done for ostentation, but everything for public utility." A similar view on the desirability of stable laws was held by Aristotle and Thomas Aquinas. Huntington Cairns, *Legal Philosophy from Plato to Hegel*, 98, 194. Thomas Jefferson was of the same opinion. Dumbauld, "Thomas Jefferson and American Constitutional Law," *Journal of Public Law*, Vol. II, No. 2 (Fall, 1953), 381.

[21] "[N]ulla dos feminis: probitas cuique maritum dabat." *Historia Gotthorum*, 66; Dovring, 397. Commenting on Dig. XXIV, 1, 1 restricting interspousal transfers of property, Grotius says "quod gratuitus amor esse debeat, non emptus." *Florum Sparsio*, 169.

[22] See generally *Historia Gotthorum*, 66; Dovring, 397.

The speedy march of judicial procedure was another feature which contrasted favorably with the interminable delays characteristic of the Roman system. The comparative mildness of criminal punishments—only the gravest offenses were subject to the death penalty—likewise won the Dutch jurist's approval.[23]

Possibly a renewed interest in Roman law, which was aroused in connection with this comparison with Germanic law, led Grotius to undertake the *Florum Sparsio*. Apparently the earliest mention of the book is in a letter to his brother Willem in 1641.[24] Grotius there says, *"Florum Sparsio* [strewing of flowers] (for so I have in mind to call this adjunct to what others have given, and Godofredus[25] has collected) on the law of Justinian is finished."[26]

Two weeks later he sent to Willem the poem which was

[23] "Probo & hoc quod non vilis civium sanguis, nec nisi gravissima capite luebantur, quodque damnatorum bona salva erant liberis." *Historia Gotthorum*, 67; Dovring, 398.

[24] In this letter Grotius also voices the urgent feeling which he often expressed that publication of his writings be completed during his lifetime, under Willem's supervision, as the conduct of his sons was unsatisfactory, and he did not wish to depend upon his heirs for publication of his works. *Epistolae*, 906, 912, 914, 934, 938. See also *Schets*, 129–30.

[25] Grotius is here referring to Gothofredus, *Corpus Juris Civilis in IIII Partes Distinctum*. This annotated edition of the *Corpus Juris* was published at Geneva in 1583 by Denis Godefroy (1549–1622), an eminent jurist of that place. See *Bibliographie*, 369. Grotius praised him as the best expounder of civil law ("Gothofredus est Iuris civilis optimus monstrator"). *Epistolae*, 79. See also *Epistolae*, 716. His son Theodore came to France and had diplomatic dealings with Grotius. *Sparsa Collecta*, 414–23.

[26] "Florum sparsio (ita appellare hanc adjectiunculam ad ea quae dedere alii, quaeque collegit Godofredus visum est) ad Ius Iustinianeum absoluta est & habet quaterniones in octavo meae id est minutae literae, xxix." *Epistolae*, 924.

to serve as a preface to the *Florum Sparsio.*[27] The manuscript was completed[28] by the work of three copyists[29] and
printed with all deliberate speed.[30] Before the end of 1642
the author had sent copies to his brother,[31] and was already
completing his annotations on the New Testament by
writing on the book of Revelation. Early in 1643 he had
shipped copies to market, but feared that the vessels had
been detained by contrary winds.[32] He feared that some
copies might have fallen into the hands of the people of

[27] *Epistolae*, 925. Van Eysinga calls this an "aardige gedichtje."
Schets, 129.

[28] "Nostra ad jus descripta sunt in quarto." *Epistolae*, 933.

[29] "Florum sparsio describetur, ubi Biblica nostra descripta erunt,
in quibus jam tres uno tempore laborant, domesticus unus, duo ex-
tranei." *Epistolae*, 926.

[30] "Nostra ad jus male dixi in Octavo edi. Eduntur enim in quarto:
& pervenimus ad secundum G. nec longe absumus a fine Pandectarum.
Ad Codicem & Novellas pauca sunt." *Epistolae*, 941. "Nostra ad jus
intra mensem, puto, prodibunt." *Epistolae*, 943.

[31] Of five copies sent by way of Rouen, one was for Willem and
the others for scholarly friends of Grotius. "Mitto Rotomagum & inde
ad te exempla quinque anthobolias nostrae ad jus Iustinianeum: rogo
eam compingi pro me cures: sumasque unum tibi, alia des Vossio, Stri-
deno, Graswinckelio & Constantino Empereur." *Epistolae*, 944. Send-
ing another presentation copy on the same day, Grotius described the
work as a "munusculum philologika ad jus Iustinianaeum." *Epistolae*, 711. Later Grotius wrote to Willem: "Florum sparsio spero ad
vos venerit." *Epistolae*, 946.

[32] "Libri chartae optimae Florum sparsionis pridem a me missi
fuere Rhotomagum: sed audio nautas ventis adversantibus detineri.
Duo chartae vulgaris dedi Germano nobili Levetornario." *Epistolae*,
947. A week later he wrote: "Scripsimus Rhotomagum ut sciamus
quid sit. Gaudeo tibi laborem hunc videri non inamoenum. Vtilem
vix ausim dicere. Sunt enim flores tantum, quod ipsum profiteor. Duo
sequioris chartae exemplaria portabit vobis Lutzavius . . . Treseliani
libros melioris chartae Florum Sparsionis dedere nautae Petro Cor-
nelii Boer, ut perferret ad Hulftii nostri matrem." *Epistolae*, 947, 948.

Dunkirk, who were "not suitable readers of such things."[33]

Grotius realized that his book was more ornamental than useful to practicing lawyers.[34] Readers derived pleasure, rather than benefit, from it.[35] Yet he longed to know what erudite critics thought of it.[36] Doubtless because of its purely decorative character it has seldom been cited and is one of the least-known writings of Grotius.[37]

[33] "Florum sparsionis exemplaria melioris chartae per quem nautam ad Hulftii matrem missa sint, nuper ad te scripsi, & metuere me, ne ad Dunquercanos, non idoneos talium lectores, ista pervenerint." *Epistolae*, 948.

[34] "Liber noster est quidem non valde utilis ad res forenses: sed habet delectationis aliquid: & quanquam non nimis magni eum facio, puto rectius factum quod prodiit, quam si periisset." *Epistolae*, 948. On September 14, 1641, he had writen to Gerard Vos: "Habe & anthobolian Philosophicam, Historicam, Philologicam, ad Ius Iustinianaeum." *Epistolae*, 689.

[35] "Florum sparsio ut arbitror, non tantum utilitatis, quantum voluptatis adferet lectoribus." *Epistolae*, 949. He noted that it was being reprinted at Amsterdam: "Video recudi Florum sparsionem Amstelodami. Rogo per amicos operam des errata ut corrigantur, & ne admittantur nova." *Epistolae*, 949.

[36] "Quid de floribus nostris censeant eruditi, avebo discere." *Epistolae*, 950.

[37] Two editions were published in Amsterdam in 1643, and one in Halle in 1729, with preface by George Christian Gebauer, which was reissued in Naples in 1777 with notes by Gabriel Somma, a theologian of that place. *Bibliographie*, 368–70. No translation from the Latin into any other language has ever been made. This may be compared with the 112 items devoted in that *Bibliographie* to editions and translations of *De Jure Belli ac Pacis. Bibliographie*, 222–301. Most biographers of Grotius merely list the *Florum Sparsio* among his writings. Brandt and van Cattenburgh, *Historie van het Leven des Heeren Huig de Groot*, II, 297, 440–43 (calling it, in Dutch, *bloemstrooijing*); Vreeland, *Hugo Grotius*, 236 (calling it "Remarks on Justinian's Laws"); Knight, 292 (merely listing it); *Schets*, 129 (describing it as "los darheen als bloemen geworpen aanteekeningen op het Corpus juris").

II.

The characterization of the *Florum Sparsio* given in his correspondence is corroborated by the prefatory poem[38] which he placed at the front of the book. These ten lines read:

> *Non ego sub quorum pendent examine causae,*
> *Non ego pro trepidis ora diserta reis,*
> *Non ego dictantes legum praescripta magistros*
> *Quicquam, quod sit opus scire, docere volo.*
> *Hoc faciant, adolens Themidis Cujacius aram,*
> *Ingentique bono nomina natae, Fabri.*[39]
> *At si quis latebrosa terens aenigmata legum*
> *Pectora de tetrico fessa labore refert,*
> *Hunc ego solabor. det ditior alter aristas*
> *Pomaque. Nos Flores, munera parua, damus.*[40]

Grotius emphasizes that it is for others to bring rich gifts

[38] Notes 27, 31, 32, 34, and 35, above.

[39] Grotius praised Peter Faber and recommended to students of Roman law all the works of the celebrated French jurist Cujas (1522–90). "Caetera huc pertinentia vide apud Petrum Fabrum, cuius librum ad iuris Regulas, vt & Cuiacij omnia, Romani iuris studiosis eximie commendo." *Florum Sparsio,* 321–22.

[40] In *Epistolae* "nota" appears as a variant for "natae" in the sixth line, and seems to be a better reading. We translate the poem as follows: "I do not wish to teach anything which it is necessary for those to know who have cases under their examination, or who orate eloquently on behalf of anxious defendants, or who as magistrates dictate the precepts of the laws. Let Cujas do that, worshipping at the altar of Themis the goddess of justice, and the Fabri, names known for great good. But if anyone winnowing the hidden mysteries of the laws comes back with heart weary from the severe labor, I shall console him. Let another richer one give sheaves of grain and fruit. We give flowers, small presents." *Epistolae,* 925.

such as ears of corn and fruit; he gave but a small present of flowers.[41] Examination of the structure of the book confirms this analysis. Using Justinian's *Corpus Juris* as a framework, Grotius collects passages from ancient historians, orators, poets, and legal commentators which illustrate the meaning of words and phrases used in the laws. In the *Law of War and Peace* Grotius had used material of the same kind, as well as Biblical references;[42] but there he had been assembling authorities to establish the validity of the legal propositions which he was enunciating. Here, in the *Florum Sparsio,* he had no polemic purpose. He was not an advocate seeking to prove the correctness of any doctrinal assertions, but was merely gathering data to demonstrate the usage of words occurring in the *Corpus Juris.*[43]

One might illustrate the different technique used by Grotius in the two works by imagining a volume entitled

[41] These verses bring to mind the lines of an American poet, Edna St. Vincent Millay:

> No gracious weight of golden fruits to sell
> Have I, nor any wise and wintry thing.

She also pictures a moribund monarch:

> Rising on elbow in the dark to sing
> Some rhyme now out of season but well known
> In days when banners in his face were blown
> And every woman had a rose to fling.

Millay, *The Harp-Weaver and Other Poems,* 56, 66.

[42] See pp. 30–31, 76, above.

[43] Apart from his following the sequence established by the *Corpus Juris* rather than an alphabetical order, the technique used by Grotius is similar to that employed in compiling a modern unabridged dictionary, which gives a series of examples showing the earliest and later use of a particular word or expression. Appropriately enough, Grotius devotes lengthy discussion to the *Digest* title "De verborum significatione." *Florum Sparsio,* 279–305.

A *Strewing of Flowers upon the Constitution of the United States*. The work would begin:

We, the People of the United States] President Abraham Lincoln spoke of government *of the people, by the people, for the people*. Gettysburg Address, *in fine*. On another occasion he said *You can fool some of the people all the time, and all the people some of the time, but you can't fool all the people all the time*. The poet Archibald MacLeish wrote that any political achievement would be possible *if the people wished*. A *Time to Speak*, p. 3. The Virginia statesman Thomas Jefferson declared that reasons should be given when it became *necessary for one people to dissolve the political bands which have connected them with another*. Declaration of Independence, *in principio*. Jefferson's rival in President George Washton's cabinet, the financier Alexander Hamilton, once exclaimed, *The people, sir, is a great beast*.

In order to form a more perfect union] The celebrated Massachusetts orator Daniel Webster spoke of *liberty and union, now and forever, one and inseparable*. Reply to Hayne. So too the New England poet Henry Wadsworth Longfellow sang *Sail on, O union strong and great!* The Building of the Ship. President Jefferson believed that *Every measure should be taken which may draw the bands of union tighter*. To John Brown, May 26, 1788. When the Missouri Question arose he *considered it at once as the knell of the union*. To John Holmes, April 22, 1820. He declared that *union is second in my wishes to no other principle but that of living under a republican government*. To Gilbert Merritt, July 10, 1821. President Andrew Jackson proclaimed: *The union! It must and shall be preserved*. Toast.[44]

[44] It is hoped that the difference in Grotius' technique in the two works is illustrated by the contrast between this method of com-

Since the skeleton or framework upon which Grotius hangs (or at which he hurls) his floral tribute is Justinian's *Corpus Juris*, it will be proper to analyze briefly that landmark of legal genius.

Like many illustrious examples of legal writing, it appeared late in the history of the legal system which it adorned, and in fact might be regarded as a death mask of the era which it epitomized. In England Blackstone's famous *Commentaries*[45] likewise drew a perfect portrait of a body of law which was about to disappear. American lawyers, framing the Constitution of the United States along lines derived from notions of the English Constitution popularized by Blackstone and Montesquieu,[46] perpetuated features that were already moribund in the land of their origin.[47]

When Justinian's legislative chef-d'oeuvre appeared, the Roman republic had been destroyed,[48] and indeed the Roman Empire had been divided and was partially defunct. The Western Empire is generally regarded as ending in 476 A.D. The Eastern or Byzantine Empire continued until the capture of Constantinople by the Turks in 1453 A.D. Justinian's *Corpus Juris* may be considered as completed in 534 A.D.[49]

---

piling a commentary on the Constitution and that adopted in Dumbauld, *The Constitution of the United States*, 59.

[45] Sir William Blackstone, *Commentaries on the Laws of England*.

[46] Charles Louis de Montesquieu, *L'Esprit des Lois*.

[47] Such as the power of the king to veto legislation.

[48] See John Dickinson, *Death of a Republic*, 237–38. The Twelve Tables from 450 B.C. are perhaps the earliest remaining landmark of Roman law.

[49] Like any extensive enterprise, such as publication of the *Papers*

The *Corpus Juris* is divided into four major parts. The first of these is the *Institutes,* comprising four books. These constitute an elementary textbook for legal instruction. The first book deals with the law of persons. Next comes the law of things, covering the acquisition and loss of various kinds of property rights. The law of obligations is then treated, including the various forms of contracts known in Roman law, as well as obligations arising *ex delicto* (or torts, as they are called in Anglo-American law). Finally the law of actions (*actiones,* or legal remedies and procedure) is set forth.[50]

The *Institutes* followed the model of an earlier similar treatise by the jurist Gaius, and served in turn as the model for the *Introduction to Dutch Jurisprudence,* by Grotius, and for Blackstone's *Commentaries on the Laws of England* (and doubtless for countless other analytical treatises dealing with various systems of law).[51]

The second (and most voluminous and important) part of the *Corpus Juris* is known as the *Digests* (or *Pandects*).

of Thomas Jefferson, the preparation of Justinian's legislation actually covered a long period of time. Justinian began his reign in 527. A commission was appointed in 528 to begin the work. The first version of the *Code* was issued in 529. On November 15, 534, the revised *Code* was enacted, effective December 29, 534. The *Institutes* had been enacted November 21, 533, effective December 30, 533. The *Digests* were enacted December 16, 533, effective December 30, 533. The first *Novellae,* or new enactments, which became part of the traditional *Corpus Juris,* were published in 538.

[50] Grotius recognized that an action was itself a species of property. "Sed & actio ipsa res est, & in bonis esse dicitur." *Florum Sparsio,* 295. Similarly, American constitutional law before the "New Deal" era treated contracts as being property rights. Roscoe Pound, "Liberty of Contract," *Yale Law Journal,* Vol. XVIII, No. 7, (May, 1909), 454, 461.

[51] See p. 128, above.

The *Digests* contain, in fifty books, a collection of extracts from the writings of celebrated jurists whose views were regarded as authoritative.[52] A statute of 426 A.D. gave force to opinions of Ulpianus, Paulus, Papinianus, Gaius, and Modestinus. Questions were to be decided in accordance with the views of a majority of these jurists; if there were no majority with respect to the controverted issue, the side on which Papinianus stood was to prevail. If there were still no answer, the official dealing with the case was obliged to determine the law for himself.[53] Passages from the writings of Ulpian make up approximately one-third of the *Digests*; about half as much is from Paulus. The *Institutes* and *Digests* constitute what may be regarded as the common law or the "taught law"[54] of the Roman legal system.

The *Digests*, containing the elaborated details of the

[52] Under the complex Roman system of judicial procedure, litigants applied to the "praetor" (a public official having *imperium*, or exercising the sovereign political power) for a *formula* establishing the facts to be proved and the legal consequences thereof. The *judex* (a judge of fact, like our jury) applied the *formula* and determined whether the facts set forth therein as determinative of the legal rights of the parties had been adequately proved. In framing the *formula* the views of learned jurists regarding the law were taken into account by the praetor. As early as 67 B.C. the *lex Cornelia* made the opinions of qualified jurists (responsa prudentium) binding upon the praetor. In 125 A.D. the provisions of the perpetual edict of Salvius Julianus were made binding. Augustus licensed *responsa* by certain jurists, and Hadrian made them binding on the praetor. *Institutes*, I, 2, 8; *Digests*, I, 2, 49.

[53] Roscoe Pound, *Readings in Roman Law*, 8; Gray, *Nature and Sources of the Law*, 264–65. See also Adolf Berger, *Encyclopedic Dictionary of Roman Law*.

[54] In Maitland's familiar phrase: "taught law is tough law." Frederic William Maitland, *English Law and the Renaissance*, 18.

reasoning of the jurists whose writings are quoted,[55] form the most significant part of the *Corpus Juris*.[56]

The *Code*, or third part of the *Corpus Juris*, contains a collection of *constitutiones*[57] (statutory enactments by the emperors). In these arbitrary provisions of legislation by the emperors the conflicting and confusing determinations to which Grotius referred in his *Historia Gotthorum* are mostly to be found.

Traditionally treated as the fourth part of the *Corpus Juris* (though not, of course, included in the original *Code*) were the *Novellae*, or new *constitutiones* embodying legistion subsequently formulated by Justinian up to the date of his death in 565 A.D. (These may be thought of as similar to the pocket supplements to the compilations of legislation familiar to American lawyers today.)

During the Middle Ages scholars annotated the traditional text of the *Corpus Juris* with their own glosses. Thus the twelfth and thirteenth centuries are known as the pe-

---

[55] In the three-volume Mommsen, Krüger, Schoell, and Kroll edition (15th ed., Berlin, 1928) commonly used by scholars today, the *Institutes* occupy 56 pages, the *Digests* 897, the *Code* 483, and the *Novellae* 803. In *Florum Sparsio*, Grotius devotes to the *Institutes* 66 pages, to the *Digests* 249, to the *Code* 78, and to the *Novellae* 12. These pages embrace 203, 741, 341, and 49 items or paragraphs respectively. Note 30, above.

[56] Hence, one speaks of the *usus modernus pandectarum* when referring to the use of Roman law in the local law of the nations that arose in modern times from the ruins of the Roman Empire. The *Pandects* or *Digests* are used by metonymy to signify the entire *Corpus Juris*. For the medieval divisions of the Corpus Juris, see Sir William S. Holdsworth, *History of English Law*, II, 136–37.

[57] For a definition of *constitutio*, see *Institutes*, I, 2, 6; *Digests*, 1, 4, 1, 1.

riod of the glossators.[58] Of these the most celebrated
were the so-called "four doctors": Bulgarus, Martinus,
Jacobus, and Hugo. Later Accursius compiled a composite
gloss which thereafter was accepted as the *glossa ordinaria*
or definitive version.

Since part of the *Corpus Juris* was in Greek, and since
much of the actual law in force in Rome during classical
times had little rational relevance to medieval conditions
under feudalism,[59] two rules were followed which simpli-
fied the work of medieval jurists: *Graeca non leguntur*[60]
and *quidquid non agnoscit glossa, id non agnoscit curia.*[61]

The acceptance in local law of the *Corpus Juris* as inter-
preted by legal scholars is known as the "reception of
Roman law." Because English law after Henry II had become a homogeneous system of law enforced by the central
government through the royal courts, Roman law was
never received en masse in England.[62]

A fortiori, it was never received in the United States,
although it is sometimes said[63] that there was a distinct
possibility of such reception during the latter part of the

[58] The succeeding period is known as that of the "post-glossators"
or "commentators." See Holdsworth, *History of English Law*, IV,
220–21, 243.

[59] The problem is similar to the adoption of English common
law in the United States. See Zechariah Chafee, Jr., "Colonial
Courts and the Common Law," *Proceedings of the Mass. Historical
Society*, Vol. LXVIII (1952), 132; Ford W. Hall, "The Common
Law—An Account of Its Reception in the United States," *Vander-
bilt Law Review*, Vol. IV, No. 4 (June, 1951), 791, 798–800.

[60] What is in Greek is not read.

[61] What is not known in the gloss is not known by the court.

[62] Maitland, *English Law and the Renaissance*, 35; William Stubbs,
Seventeen Lectures on the Study of Medieval and Modern History,
157; Holdsworth, *History of English Law*, IV, 285–86.

[63] Roscoe Pound, *The Formative Era of American Law*, 107.

eighteenth century. At that time political antipathy to England led to prohibiting the citation of modern English judicial decisions.[64] Learned American lawyers such as Kent and Story were familiar with European treatises on civil law and often cited them. Thomas Jefferson considered the Roman law as an expression of "written reason" superior to the cumbersome and arbitrary rules developed during the course of English history by the courts of that nation.[65]

During the nineteenth century the movement for modern codifications of national law, based upon Roman-law tradition, led to widespread legislation, such as the celebrated Code Napoléon in France. The civil-law tradition, based upon Roman law, thus stands today as the complement of the common law derived from English precedents.[66]

[64] Roscoe Pound, *The Lawyer from Antiquity to Modern Times*, 180–81; Julian S. Waterman, "Thomas Jefferson and Blackstone's Commentaries," *Illinois Law Review*, Vol. XXVII, No. 6 (Feb., 1933), 630, 644.

[65] "The lawyer finds in the Latin language the system of civil law most conformable with the principles of justice of any which has ever yet been established among men, and from which much has been incorporated into our own." *Writings of Thomas Jefferson*, XV, 210. "The Roman law, the principles of which are the nearest to natural reason, of those of any municipal code hitherto known" was relied upon in a diplomatic note to the British minister from Secretary of State Jefferson. *Works of Thomas Jefferson*, VII, 3. On other occasions Jefferson admitted "the superiority of the civil over the common law code, as a system of perfect justice" and described it as "a system carried to a degree of conformity with natural reason attained by no other." *Writings of Thomas Jefferson*, XIII, 166; XVIII, 35.

[66] Today one must add the Communist and African or oriental legal systems in order to form a complete conspectus of modern law. For an illustration of the co-operative interaction between systems, see Robert H. Jackson, "Lawyers Today: The Legal Profession in a

One of the notable features observed on reading the *Florum Sparsio* is the extent of the linguistic or textual comments made by the author. He suggested emendations to the received text of the *Corpus Juris* just as he did in connection with his editions of classical authors or his Biblical studies.[67] Another notable feature is the number of references by Grotius to his annotations on the New Testament[68] and to his *Law of War and Peace*.[69]

III.

Several matters discussed by Grotius in the *Florum Sparsio* are worthy of special mention (as *flores florum*, so to speak). First to be considered are his comments on natural law and the law of nations, topics treated in his better-known works *De Jure Belli ac Pacis* and *De Jure Praedae*.[70]

World of Paradox," *American Bar Association Journal*, Vol. XXXIII, No. 1 (Jan., 1947), 89; Jackson, "Some Problems in Developing an International Legal System," *Temple Law Quarterly*, Vol. XXII, No. 2 (Oct., 1948), 157; Jackson, "The Nuremberg Trial," in *David Dudley Field Centenary Essays*, 319.

[67] *Sparsa Collecta*, 373. Of 58 such instances, 50 occur in the *Digests*, 6 in the *Code*, and 2 in the *Novellae*. Some of the emendations of Grotius are followed in Mommsen–Krüger. See *e.g.*, *Florum Sparsio*, 202, 213.

[68] Of these, 4 occur in the *Digests*, 2 in the *Code*, and 1 in the *Novellae*. There are also references to other literary works of Grotius. *Florum Sparsio*, 10, 36, 231. Grotius likewise praises Gerard Vos, "vir omnium literarum peritissimus Gerardus Vossius." *Florum Sparsio*, 314–15.

[69] Of 56 citations to *De Jure Belli ac Pacis*, 10 occur in the *Institutes*, 42 in the *Digests*, 3 in the *Code*, and 1 in the *Novellae*. See p. 179, below.

[70] See pp. 37–40 and 62–64, above.

In commenting on the passage "Natural law is what nature has taught all animals,"[71] Grotius writes:

Why we think this accepted distribution of law into law of nature and law of nations is less philosophical, we have set forth in *De Jure Belli ac Pacis.*[72] . . . And so law is more rightly divided into that which exists by nature, and is manifest of its own force (*per se*) to men not corrupted; and into that which is positively constituted [established by the will of a legislator], which in turn is either common to many nations by ancient custom, or peculiar to a particular state, whether it rests upon laws or usages.[73]

Those rules which are called laws of nature are rightly ascribed to God.[74]

Further on,[75] Grotius explains that in the passage of the *Digests* then under discussion, the "civil law" was be-

[71] "Ius naturale est quod natura omnia animalia docuit," *Digests,* I, 1, 3.

[72] I, i, 9 and 11. The erudite English jurist John Selden is cited as agreeing with Grotius.

[73] "Cur hanc distributionem iuris in ius naturae & gentium sic acceptum minus esse philosophicam putemus, diximus nos. 1. *de iure Belli ac Pacis,* cap. I, §.9. & 11. Dixit & eruditissime, vt solet, Seldenus, de iure naturae & gentium, secundum Hebraeos. Itaque rectius ius diuiditur in id quod natura est, & per se hominibus non corruptis patet: & in id quod est ex constituto: quod rursum est aut multis gentibus commune ex consuetudine antiqua, aut proprium ciuitatis cuiusque, siue id legibus, siue moribus constet." *Florum Sparsio,* 77. See also p. 62, above, and p. 172, below.

[74] "Eas vero, quae naturae dicuntur leges recte Deo asscribi, & nos in prolegomenis de iure Belli ac Pacis, librique primi capite primo ostendimus, & late Origines libro quinto contra Celsum." *Florum Sparsio,* 20. See also pp. 40, 63, above.

[75] Commenting on *Digests,* L, 16, 10.

ing used in contrast to "equity,"[76] rather than as distinguished from the law of nations. For the law of nations, Grotius observed, "is included in the civil law to the extent that it is adopted and confirmed by the civil law" of a particular nation.[77]

In commenting on a passage at the beginning of the *Digests* where a division of law into three categories is mentioned,[78] Grotius says:

If you look at it attentively, our jurisconsults have divided many things into three parts, because that number is believed to have something divine about it. In other respects, if one wished to set up an accurate division, he might easily divide any class (genus) whatever into two parts, and each of these again into two. Thus law either exists by nature or is laid down [by a lawgiver as positive law]. That laid down is either law of nations or civil law. Law is public or private: that which is public relates to sacred or profane things. The precepts of the law look toward general or special justice: to special justice either by forbidding or by commanding. Law pertains either to persons or to those things which are outside the person. Outside the person are things (res) and ac-

[76] The strict civil law (*jus civile*) was that governing nothing but the relations of Roman citizens *inter sese* (the *jus Quiritium*). This was modified by the equitable principles introduced through the power of the praetor and set forth in the edict which he issued at his inauguration in office. Later the edict was made perpetual, and binding on the praetor and his successors. In 342 A.D. the difference between law and equity was abolished, as in the Federal Rules of Civil Procedure. *Code*, II, 57, 1. Note 52, above.

[77] "Ius ciuile hic honorario opponitur, non iuri gentium, quod comprehenditur sub iure ciuili, quatenus a iure ciuili firmatur." *Florum Sparsio*, 286.

[78] *Digests*, I, 2, 2, 38. See also *Institutes*, I, 1, 4.

tions (actiones). Persons are free or servile. Free persons
are born free or freedmen, and so on.[79]

In recommending this system of dichotomous classification, did Grotius anticipate the binary functioning of
present-day computers?

In a vein comparable to Lord Bacon,[80] Grotius quotes
from Pliny[81] an admonition that patience is the duty of
a judge, for it is a great part of justice.[82] In another place
he emphasizes, by a quotation from Seneca,[83] the necessity

[79] "Si recte aduertas, pleraque iurisconsulti nostri in tria diuisere,
quod is numerus aliquid diuini habere crederetur. Alioqui, si quis
accuratum sectionem instituere volet, facile genus quodque in duo
secabit, & horum alterum rursum in duo. Sic ius est natura aut positione. Positione gentium aut ciuile. Ius est publicum aut priuatum:
publicum in sacris, in profanis. Praecepta iuris aut ad iustitiam spec-
tant generalem aut specialem: ad specialem vetando, iubendo. Perti-
net ius ad personas, aut ea quae extra personam sunt: extra personam sunt res & actiones. Personae sunt liberae aut seruiles. Liberae
ingenuae aut libertinae: & ita de caeteris." *Florum Sparsio,* 82.

[80] Francis Bacon, *Essays,* 254. "Patience and gravity of hearing
is an essential part of justice; and an overspeaking judge is no well-
tuned cymbal. It is no grace to a judge first to find that which he
might have heard in due time from the bar; or to show quickness of
conceit in cutting off evidence or counsel too short; or to prevent
information by questions, though pertinent. The parts of a judge
in hearing are four: to direct the evidence; to moderate length, repetition, or impertinency of speech; to recapitulate, select, and collate
the material points of that which hath been said; and to give the rule
or sentence. Whatsoever is above these is too much; and proceedeth
either of glory and willingness to speak, or of impatience to hear, or
of shortness of memory, or of want of a staid and equal attention."

[81] The reference may be found in Pliny, *Epistles,* VI, Ep. ii, 8.
See also Selatie E. Stout (ed.), *Plinius Epistulae,* 169.

[82] "Iudex patientiam debeat, quae pars magna iustitiae est."
Florum Sparsio, 103.

[83] "Qui statuit aliquid, parte inaudita altera, Aequum licet sta-
tuerit, haud aequus fuit." Seneca, *Medea,* lines 199–200.

of hearing both sides of a case and not judging ex parte.[84] On the other side of the coin, he points out that disrespect to a magistrate is disrespect to the state itself.[85]

Grotius makes a number of comments that have a modern ring, and could be cited in support of recent decisions respecting the constitutional rights of persons accused of crime. For example, he recognizes the untrustworthiness of confessions which are not made voluntarily.[86]

Something resembling the right to a public trial (guaranteed by the sixth amendment)[87] is suggested by the comment[88] of Grotius that "Solon wished that the trial of injuries should be public, that is, that anyone be admitted as accuser, because it is as if in one citizen the liberty of all is despised."[89]

The notion, congenial to Americans, that law should be based on common consent,[90] is also to be found in Grotius.

[84] *Florum Sparsio,* 236.

[85] "Qui enim Magistratum spernit, ciuitatem spernit, vt ait Aristoteles." *Florum Sparsio,* 232. Thus in English law it was treason to slay one of the king's judges. Dumbauld, *The Constitution of the United States,* 374.

[86] "Et haec quidem ad confessiones sponte factas pertinent. Nam illis quae per tormenta, quam periculosum sit indiscrete credere, ostendit insignis historia apud Philostratum in vita Apollonij v. 8 . . . Notum illud Mimi: Saepe innocentem cogit mentiri dolor." *Florum Sparsio,* 218, commenting on *Digests,* XLII, 2.

[87] Dumbauld, *The Bill of Rights and What It Means Today,* 53, 67.

[88] On *Digests,* XLVII, 10.

[89] "Solon iniuriarum publicum voluit esse iudicium, id est, quemuis admitti accusatorem, quod in vno ciue quasi omnium contemnatur libertas." *Florum Sparsio,* 231. Grotius really means by public trial an *actio popularis* where anyone may sue on behalf of the public. On English law see Wroth and Zobel, *Legal Papers of John Adams,* III, 254.

[90] Dumbauld, *The Declaration of Independence and What It Means Today,* 67–74.

Commenting on the definition "Law is a common precept,"[91] Grotius says: "This definition, indeed, seems particularly to have regard to a popular state: nevertheless it can also be adapted to the constitutions of monarchs, where the power of the monarchs arises from the consent of the people."[92]

The present-day "rule of law" movement might appropriately quote the translation by Grotius of the statement of Dion Chrysostomus[93] that "Law is the guide of life."[94]

Recent American constitutional decisions have emphasized the Jeffersonian principle that the state should punish wrongful acts, not ideas or thoughts.[95] Early Roman law adopted the contrary principle that "in crimes the intent, not the event, is regarded."[96] But, as Grotius notes approvingly, the later trend was to limit this principle to the crime of treason.[97] Commenting on a *Code* provision that "the laws wished criminal intent to be punished with

[91] "Lex est commune praeceptum," *Digests*, I, 3, 1.

[92] "Quae definitio proprie quidem popularem statum respicere videtur: potest tamen & principum constitutionibus aptari, vbi principum potestas ex populi consensu nata est." *Florum Sparsio*, 83. See p. 65, n. 51, above. Compare the familiar passage *Institutes*, I. 2, 6 and *Digests*, I, 4, 1, pr.

[93] The reference may be found in Dio's 75th Discourse, rather than the 76th as cited by Grotius. *Dio Chrysostom with an English Translation by H. Lamar Crosby*, V, 240.

[94] "Lex vitae dux est." *Florum Sparsio*, 84.

[95] Dumbauld, *The Bill of Rights and What It Means Today*, 111. See also Grotius, *Law of War and Peace*, II, xx, 18.

[96] "In maleficiis voluntas spectatur, non exitus." *Digests*, XLVIII, 8, 14. Grotius comments on this passage in *Florum Sparsio*, 247.

[97] Compare Holdsworth, *History of English Law*, III, 292–93, 373. As to treason in American law, see Dumbauld, *The Constitution of the United States*, 374.

THE LIFE AND LEGAL WRITINGS OF HUGO GROTIUS

the same severity as the effect of a crime,"[98] Grotius writes:
"This was well said of the early Roman law, where in the
case of crimes, especially the more serious offenses, even
evil thoughts, not yet consummated, were punished, the
mind being bloody though the hand be clean. . . . But a
later age restricted this almost exclusively to the crime
of treason."[99] Emperor Tiberius said that "in a free state
tongues should be free."[100]

A curious feature of Roman criminal law was the fact
that being a "mathematician" (*mathematicus*) was a crime.
The term was used to designate an astrologer or fortune-
teller. Justinian was severe in punishing these offenders. It
was a capital offense to consult astrologers concerning the
health of the monarch.[101]

Perennial interest attaches to the problem discussed by
Grotius regarding the possible rehabilitation of criminals.
Penologists and judges today at their seminars on sentencing[102] might well bear in mind the passage from Plutarch
which Grotius quotes: "Some vices are curable, others in-

[98] "Eadem enim severitate voluntatem sceleris qua effectum puniri
iura voluerunt." *Code*, IX, 8, 5.

[99] "Bene hoc dictum ex vetere iure Romano, quo in maleficiis,
nempe grauioribus, etiam cogitata mala, non perfecta adhuc, vindi-
cabantur, cruenta mente, pura manu. . . . Sed hoc posterior aetas
ferme ad solum retraxit crimen maiestatis." *Florum Sparsio*, 379,
380. *Ibid.*, 377.

[100] "In ciuitate libera, liberas linguas esse debere." *Florum Sparsio*,
378.

[101] "Graue crimen, si probetur." *Florum Sparsio*, 384–85. Compare
the English law on imagining the King's death, Holdsworth, *History of English Law*, III, 292, and on witchcraft, *ibid.*, IV, 507–11.

[102] See *Papers Delivered at the Institute on Sentencing for United
States District Judges*, 35 F.R.D. 381 (1964). Likewise of interest
today are the questions whether penalties should be prescribed spe-
cifically by law or left to the discretion of the sentencing judge. "Duae
hic quaestiones oriri possunt: prior est, rectiusne poenae omnes

curable. The rod corrects those who can be changed for the better, the axe cuts off that which can not be corrected."[103]

There is a modern ring also in what Grotius says about collection of revenue by the public treasury. Commenting on a provision in the *Digests* that says, "I do not consider him to be delinquent who in doubtful questions gave a ready answer adverse to the treasury,"[104] Grotius remarks: "The cause of the treasury is never a bad one except under a good ruler."[105]

Grotius believed that philosophers and lawyers should not bring suit for fees; not because their services are not valuable, but because it is unworthy of their high calling to set store upon pecuniary reward.[106]

iudicum permittantur arbitrio, an definiantur legibus. . . . Altera est, an iudices minores legibus poenas constituere possint, non iam dico in casibus, in quibus leges ipsae id permittunt, sed generaliter." *Florum Sparsio*, 256. The same question was pondered in Puritan New England. George L. Haskins, *Law and Authority in Early Massachusetts*, 117.

[103] "Vitia alia sunt sanabilia, alia insanabilia: virgae eos corrigunt, qui in melius mutari possunt: secures praecidunt, id quod corrigi non potest." *Florum Sparsio*, 256. Grotius refers in this connection to his discussion of penal law in *De Jure Belli ac Pacis*, Book II, chapter 20. See note 12, above. He also observes that much unchristian conduct is not punished by law. "Multa sunt legibus impunita, quae cum Christi regulis pugnant." *Florum Sparsio*, 262. The reference of Plutarch (*Roman Questions*, 82) may be found in *Plutarch's Moralia* (trans. by Frank Cole Babbitt), IV, 124.

[104] "Non puto delinquere eum, qui in dubiis quaestionibus contra fiscum facile responderit." *Digests*, XLIX, 14, 10.

[105] "Fisci causa mala non est nisi sub bono Principe." *Florum Sparsio*, 265. Grotius adds that Marcus Antoninus the Philosopher was such a ruler, and did not favor the treasury in his decisions.

[106] "Egregie dicta haec: non quod non philosophiam docentibus multum debeamus, sed quod indignum sit philosopho, vt & iurisconsulto, mercedem petere." *Florum Sparsio*, 275–76.

Regarding monopolies, Grotius held that they were of two kinds. Monopolies of the necessities of life are rightly regarded as odious. But monopolies of articles that serve more for pleasure (such as spices) are permissible.[107]

In conclusion, it may be said that the oblivion that has enveloped this little-known work by Grotius is perhaps justifiable. The book is ornamental rather than practical in character. The author reverts to his early aspirations as a man of letters rather than as a man of law.[108] In comparison with his other solid legal writings, it may fittingly be said of this delightful and decorative volume: "Without the help of genius, erudition is vain."[109]

[107] "Monopolia duorum sunt generum: alia rerum necessariarum vitae, quae merito sunt odiosa. . . . Alterum est genus earum rerum, quae voluptati magis seruiunt, vt erinaceorum, & Indicarum mercium, de quibus diximus II. de iure Belli ac Pacis XII. 14. & in Annotatis." *Florum Sparsio*, 357. Grotius here adheres to the views advanced in 1613 during a diplomatic dispute between the Dutch and English regarding trade with the Indies. See also Grotius, *War and Peace*, II, ii, 24; *Schets*, 47.

[108] See p. 7, above.

[109] "Ni ingenium adiuuet, imbecillem esse eruditionem." *Florum Sparsio*, 82.

Following is a list of references in *Florum Sparsio* to Grotius' earlier and more famous work, *De Jure Belli ac Pacis*. The first figure in each citation is the page in *Florum Sparsio* on which the reference appears; next is given the book, chapter, and section of *De Jure Belli ac Pacis*. In parentheses is the page reference to the 1939 varorium edition of B.J.A. de Kanter–van Hettinga Tromp.

Institutes

13: III, x (731); 20: Prol. (12); I, i (35); 23: II, 27 [I, i, 2–7] (30–32); 27: II, v, 7 (233); 38: II, viii, 3 (297); 39: III, vi, 8 (686); 45: II, viii, 7 (299); 59: II, vii, 6 (298); 67: III, xi, 14 (757).

Digests

77: I, i, 9 & 11 (34, 37); 78: II, xxii, 11 (559); 87: II, lvi, 20 (418); 95: II, xii, 26 (356); 98: III, iii, 8 (653); 121: II, v, 19 (252); 139: II, xi, 1 (326); 146: II, x, 1 (319); 148: II, xii, 3 (341); 164: III, xi, 4 (741); 176: II, vi, *in fine* (263); 208: III, xxi, 21 (859); 211: II, vi, 1 (261); viii, 25 (308); 212: III, vi, 7 (684); 213: II, viii, 9 (300); 215: II, ix, 3 (309); 220: III, xv, 9 & 10 (795, 796); 225: II, iv (219); 226: II, xii, 2 (340); 236: II, xv, 5 (391); 245: I, ii, 5 (55); 255: II, xx (462); 262: II, xix, 5 (456); 265: III, vi, 12 (688); III, ix, 14 (727); 266: III, vi, 3 (682); ix, 2 (718); I, iii, 21 (128); III, ix, 4 (719); III, vi, 12 (688); 267: III, ix, 13 (728); vi, 4 (683); 272: II, v, 17 (250); III, xx,

4 (827); 274: II, xviii (435); 287: II, xiv, 6 (381); 290: II, ix, 6 (312); 302: II, xx, 2 (464); 314: III, xxi, 4 (854).

Code

337: II, xx (462); 357: II, xii, 14 (348) [should be II, xii, 16 (350)]; 395: II, [vii, 1] (268).

Novellae

409: II, iii, 10 (209).

BIBLIOGRAPHY

Works of Grotius

No attempt will be made here to mention even the major works of Grotius in fields other than law. Such an effort would be superfluous in view of the availability of the following excellent bibliographical works:

ter Meulen, Jacob, and P. J. J. Diermanse. *Bibliographie des écrits imprimés de Hugo Grotius*. La Haye, 1950. [Lists over 1,300 items, classified into nine groups: (1) poetry; (2) philosophy and natural science; (3) philology; (4) international law; (5) history; (6) law (other than international); (7) church and state; (8) theology; (9) correspondence.]
———. *Bibliographie des écrits sur Hugo Grotius imprimés au XVIIe siècle*. La Haye, 1961.
Rogge, H. C. *Bibliotheca Grotiana*. The Hague, 1883.

Legal Writings of Grotius

Anthologia Grotiana. The Hague, 1955. [A useful collection of extracts from the writings of Grotius, with a translation into Dutch where the original is not in that language.]
de Bruyn, Daniel P. (ed.). *The Opinions of Grotius as Contained in the Hollandsche Consultatien en Advijsen*. London, 1894.

Grotius, Hugo. *De Ivre Belli ac Pacis Libri Tres.* Paris, 1625.

A handsome and useful variorum edition by B.J.A. de Kanter–van Hettinga Tromp collating the editions appearing during the lifetime of Grotius (in 1625, 1631, 1632, 1642, and 1646) was published at The Hague in 1939.

An English translation of the 1646 edition by Francis W. Kelsey and others, sponsored by the Carnegie Endowment for International Peace, bears the imprint Oxford, 1925; but Books I and II were actually issued in 1927, and Book III in 1928. A prior volume containing the Latin text appeared in 1913. See van Vollenhoven, *Verspreide Geschriften*, I, 475, 479.

A reprint of the *Prolegomena* from this translation, with an introduction by Edward Dumbauld, was published at New York in 1957.

Of particular interest is the extract (in Latin with English marginal headings) which the late Professor Benjamin M. Telders of Leyden prepared during his imprisonment by the Nazis before his death in 1945 at the Bergen-Belsen concentration camp, and which was published at The Hague in 1948. The text of Telders presents in less than 200 pages that portion of the classic work of Grotius which is relevant to what is today considered international law. See Dumbauld, Book Review, *American Journal of International Law*, Vol. XLIV (1950), 232.

———. *De Jure Praedae Commentarius.* Edited by H. G. Hamaker. The Hague, 1868.

[Dutch translation: Damsté, Onno (ed.) *Verhandel-ling over het recht op buit.* Leyden, 1934.]

[English translation: Williams, Gwladys L., and Walter H. Zeydel (eds.). *Commentary on the Law of Prize and Booty.* Washington, 1950.]

———. *Florvm Sparsio Ad Ius Ivstinianevm.* Paris, 1642.

———. *Inleiding tot de Hollandsche Rechts-geleertheyd.* The Hague, 1631.

[English translation: Lee, R. W. (ed.). *The Jurisprudence of Holland.* 2 vols. Oxford, 1926–36. (Vol. I prints on opposite pages the Dutch text of the second edition of 1631 and the English translation. Vol. II contains the editor's commentary.)]

[Latin translation: Fischer, H. F. W. D. (ed.). *Institutiones Juris Hollandici.* Haarlem, 1962.]

———. *Mare Liberum.* Amsterdam, 1609.

[English translation: Magoffin, Ralph van Deman (ed.). *The Freedom of the Seas.* New York, 1916.]

———. *Parallelon rerumpublicarum liber tertius; de moribus ingenioque populorum Atheniensium, Romanorum, Batavorum.* Edited by Johan Meerman, with a Dutch translation. 5 vols. Haarlem, 1801–1803.

———. *Hugo de Groot Over goede trouw en onbetrouw-baarheid (De Fide et Perfidia).* Edited by A. Stempels. The Hague, 1945. [Dutch version of passages on good faith from work listed in preceding item.]

———. *Verantwoordingh van de VVettelijcke Regieringh van Hollandt Ende West-Vrieslandt, Mitsgaders Eenigher nabuyrighe Provincien sulcks die Was voor de veranderingh ghevallen in den Jare xvj$^{c.}$ en xviij.* Hoorn, 1622.

[Latin version: ———. *Apologeticvs eorvm qvi Hollandiae Vvestfrisiaqve et vicinis quibusnam nationibus ex legibus praefuerunt ante mutationem quae evenit anno MDCXVIII*. Paris, 1622.]

Correspondence of Grotius

For further material on the correspondence of Grotius, see ter Meulen and Diermanse, *Bibliographie de Grotius*, 604–38.

Eekhof, Albert. "Onuitgegeven brieven van en aan Hugo Grotius," *Nederlandsch Archief voor Kerkgeschiedenis* N.S., Vol. XIX (1926), 187–204.

Epistolae Hugonis Grotii ad domum regiam Sveciae et alios Svecos omnes fere ineditae. Stockholm, 1892. [Correspondence as Swedish ambassador.]

van Gelder, H. Enno (ed.). *Lijst der uitgegeven en onuitgegeven brieven van en aan Hugo Grotius 1626–1645.* [The Hague, 1943.]

Hugonis Grotii ad Ioh. Oxenstiernam et Ioh. Adl. Salvium, et Iohannis Oxenstiernae ad Cerisantem, Epistolae ineditae. Haarlem, 1829.

Hvgonis Grotii Epistolae ad Gallos. 4th ed. Leipsig and Frankfort, 1684. [First published in Leyden, 1648.]

Hugonis Grotii Epistolae . . . ad Oxenstiernas patrem et filium . . . Haarlem, 1806.

Hvgonis Grotii . . . Epistolae quotquot reperiri potuerunt. Amsterdam, 1687. [This is the most used collection of letters from Grotius.]

Hugonis Grotii Quaedam hactenus inedita. Amsterdam, 1652.

Molhuysen, Philip C., and B. L. Meulenbroek (eds.). *Briefwisseling van Hugo Grotius.* 6 vols. to date. The

Hague, 1928–67. [This is a very important and well-edited collection of Grotius' correspondence.]

Rijkskansleren Axel Oxenstiernas skrifter och brefvexling. Vol. II, Stockholm, 1889; Vol. IV, Stockholm, 1891. [Correspondence as Swedish ambassador.]

Rogge, H. C. (ed.). *Brieven van Nicolaes van Reigersberch aan Hugo de Groot.* Amsterdam, 1901. [Letters to Grotius from his brother-in-law.]

———. (ed.). *Brieven van en aan Maria van Reigersberch* Leiden, 1902. [Letters to and from Grotius' wife.]

———. "Brieven van Hugo en Willem de Groot," *De Navorscher,* Vol. LIII (1903), 517–43. [Letters between Grotius and his brother Willem.]

———. "Mr. Johan de Haen en zijne briefwisseling met Hugo de Groot," *De Navorscher,* Vol. LIV (1904), 209–35, 281–301.

van Vollenhoven, H. (ed.) *Broeders Gevangenisse.* The Hague, 1842. [A journal of Willem de Groot, Hugo's brother, covering the period of his imprisonment at Loevestein.]

Legal and Historical
Writings about Grotius

BOOKS

Adams, John. *The Works of John Adams.* Edited by Charles Francis Adams. 10 vols. Boston, 1850–56.

Aristotle. *The Nicomachean Ethics of Aristotle.* Translated by J. E. C. Welldon. London, 1897.

Asser, Tobias M. C. *Studien op het gebied van recht en staat.* Haarlem, 1889.

Bacon, Francis. *The Essays of Francis Bacon*. Edited by Mary A. Scott. New York, 1908.

Basdevant, Jules. "Grotius," in *Les Fondateurs du Droit International*. (Edited by A. Pillet.) Paris, 1904.

Benjamin, Judah P. *A Treatise on the Law of Sales of Personal Property*. 8th ed. London, 1950. [Originally published in 1868.]

Bentham, Jeremy. *An Introduction to the Principles of Morals and Legislation*. London, 1879. [Written in 1780 and published in 1789.]

Berendsen, Anne. *Verborgenheden uit het oude Delft*. Antwerp, 1962.

van Beresteyn Eltjo A. *Iconographie van Hugo Grotius*. The Hague, 1929. [Concerning portraits of Grotius.]

Berger, Adolf. *Encyclopedic Dictionary of Roman Law*. Philadelphia, 1953.

Bertens, H. *Hugo De Groot en zijn Rechtsphilosophie*. Tilburg, 1905.

Blackstone, Sir William. *Commentaries on the Laws of England*. 4 vols. Oxford, 1765–69.

Bowen, Marjorie. *The Netherlands Display'd*. London, 1926.

Brandt, Caspar, and Adriaan van Cattenburgh. *Historie van het Leven des Heeren Huig de Groot*. 2 vols. Dordrecht and Amsterdam, 1727.

Brandt, G[eeraert]. *Historie van de Rechtspleging gehouden in de Jaeren 1618 en 1619. ontrent de dry gevangene Heeren Mr. Johan van Oldenbarnevelt Mr. Rombout Hoogerbeets Mr. Hugo de Groot*. Rotterdam, 1708.

Brierly, James L. *The Law of Nations*. Oxford, 1928.

Bryce, James. *The Holy Roman Empire*. 5th ed. New York, 1904.

Burckhardt, Walther. *Die Unvollkommenheit des Völker-rechts.* Bern, 1923.

de Burigny, Jean L. V*ie de Grotius.* 2nd ed. Amsterdam, 1804.

Burrows, Millar. *An Outline of Biblical Theology.* Phila-delphia, 1946.

Busken-Huet, Conrad. *Het Land van Rembrand.* 5th ed. 3 vols in one. Haarlem, n.d. [First published, 1882–84.]

Butler, Charles. *The Life of Hugo Grotius.* London, 1826.

Cairns, Huntington. *Legal Philosophy from Plato to Hegel.* Baltimore, 1949.

Chafee, Zechariah, Jr. *The Inquiring Mind.* New York, 1928.

von Czyhlarz, Karl. *Lehrbuch der Institutionen des Rö-mischen Rechtes.* 14th ed. Vienna, 1914.

Davis, Jefferson. *The Rise and Fall of the Confederate Gov-ernment.* 2 vols. New York, 1881.

Dickinson, John. *Death of a Republic.* New York, 1963.

———. *The Statesman's Book of John of Salisbury.* New York, 1927.

Diermanse, P J. J. *Exposition La Vie et l'Oeuvre de Gro-tius, 1583–1645.* [Paris, 1965.]

Dio Chrysostom with an English Translation by H. Lamar Crosby. Vol. V. Cambridge, Mass. 1939. [Loeb's Classi-cal Library.]

[Douglas, D.] *The Biographical History of Sir William Blackstone.* London, 1782.

Downey, Glanville. *Constantinople in the Age of Justinian.* Norman, 1960.

Dumbauld, Edward. *The Bill of Rights and What It Means Today.* Norman, 1957.

———. *The Constitution of the United States.* Norman, 1964.

———. *The Declaration of Independence and What It Means Today.* Norman, 1950.

———. *Interim Measures of Protection in International Controversies.* The Hague, 1932.

———. "*Some Modern Misunderstandings of Grotius,*" in *Volkenrechtelijke Opstellen ter ere van de hoogleraren B. M. Telders, F. M. Baron van Asbeck en J. H. W. Verzijl.* Zwolle, 1957.

Edler, Friedrich. *The Dutch Republic and the American Revolution.* Baltimore, 1911.

van Eysinga, Willem J. M. *Gids voor de Groots De Iure Belli ac Pacis.* Leiden, 1945.

———. *Huigh de Groot, Een Schets.* Haarlem, 1945.

———. *Hugo Grotius, eine Biographische Skizze.* Basel, 1952. [German translation of the preceding item.]

———. *Le 350 ième Anniversaire du De Iure Praedae Commentarius de Grotius.* [French translation of address at meeting of the Royal Dutch Academy of Sciences and Letters, March 24, 1956.]

———. *Sparsa Collecta.* Leiden, 1958. [A collection of numerous articles in periodicals.]

Figgis, John N. *Studies of Political Thought from Gerson to Grotius.* 2nd ed. Cambridge, England, 1916.

Fortuin, Hugo. *Hugo de Groot's Houding ten opzichte van Oorlog en Christendom.* Amsterdam, 1946.

———. *De natuurrechtelijke grondslagen van de Groot's volkenrecht.* The Hague, 1946.

Fruin, Robert J. *Allerliefste van Hugo de Groot.* The Hague, 1957. [A paperback reprint of his "Hugo de Groot en Maria van Reigersbergh," with correspondence from Rogge's *Brieven van en aan Maria van Reigersberch*.]

———. *The Siege and Relief of Leyden in 1574*. Translated by Elizabeth Trevelyan. The Hague, 1927. [Dutch version in *Verspreide Geschriften*, II, 385–490.]

———. *Verhooren en andere bescheiden betreffende het rechtsgeding van Hugo de Groot*. Utrecht, 1871.

———. *Verspreide Geschriften*. (Edited by P. H. Blok, P. L. Muller, and S. Muller). 11 vols. The Hague, 1900–1905.

[Godefroy, Denis]. *Corpus Juris Civilis in IIII. partes distinctum*. Geneva, 1583.

Gray, John Chipman. *The Nature and Sources of the Law*. 2nd ed. New York, 1921.

Hallema, A. *Hugo de Groot, het Delftsche orakel, 1583–1645*. 2nd ed. The Hague, 1946. [First published in 1942.]

Hartenstein, Gustav. *Darstellung der Rechtsphilosophie des Hugo Grotius*. Leipzig, 1850.

Haskins, George L. *Law and Authority in Early Massachusetts*. New York, 1960.

Higgins, A. Pearce. "The Work of Grotius and of the Modern International Lawyer," in *Studies in International Relations*, 86–103. Cambridge, England, 1928.

Holdsworth, Sir William S. *A History of English Law*. 16 vols. Boston and London, 1931–66. [Regarding this monumental work, see Frederick B. Wiener, "Holdsworth's History Finally Completed," *American Bar Association Journal*, Vol. LIII, No. 4 (Apr., 1967), 321–24.]

Hvgonis Grotii Belgarum Phoenicis manes ab iniquis obtrectationibus vindicati. 2 vols. Delft, 1727. [Possibly the work of Peter A. Lehmann. See ter Meulen and Diermanse, *Bibliographie de Grotius*, xii–xiii.]

Jackson, Robert H. "The Nuremberg Trial," in *David Dudley Field Centenary Essays*. Edited by Alison Reppy. New York, 1949.

Jefferson, Thomas. *The Papers of Thomas Jefferson*. Edited by Julian Boyd. 17 vols. to date. Princeton, 1950–.

―――. *The Works of Thomas Jefferson*. Edited by Paul L. Ford. 12 vols. New York, 1904.

―――. *The Writings of Thomas Jefferson*. Edited by Andrew A. Lipscomb and Albert E. Bergh. 20 vols. Washington, 1903–1904.

Justinian. *Corpus Juris Civilis*. Edited by Theodor Mommsen, Paul Krueger, Rudolf Schoell, and Wilhelm Kroll. 3 vols. 15th ed. Berlin, 1928.

―――. *The Digest of Justinian*. Translated by Charles H. Munro. 2 vols. Cambridge, England, 1904–1909.

―――. *The Institutes of Justinian*. Translated by J. B. Moyle. 5th ed. Oxford, 1913. [First published, 1883.]

von Kaltenborn, Carl. *Die Vorläufer des Hugo Grotius auf dem Gebiete des Ius naturae et gentium sowie der Politik im Reformationszeitalter*. Leipzig, 1848.

Kerr, Hugh T., Jr. (ed.). *A Compend of the Institutes of the Christian Religion by John Calvin*. Philadelphia, 1939.

van Kleffens, Eelco N. *Juggernaut over Holland*. New York, 1941.

Knight, W. S. M. *The Life and Works of Hugo Grotius*. London, 1925. [The most comprehensive biography of Grotius in English.]

Lowry, Charles. *Communism and Christ*. New York, 1952.

Luden, Heinrich. *Hugo Grotius nach seinen Schicksalen und Schriften dargestellt*. Berlin, 1806.

Lysen, A. (ed.). *Hugo Grotius, 1625–1925*. Leyden, 1925.

Maitland, Frederic William. *English Law and the Renaissance*. Cambridge, England, 1901.

Merula, Paulus. *Synopsis praxeos civilis, Maniere van procederen in dese provincien Hollandt, Zeeland ende West-Vriesland, belangende civile zaken*. Leyden, 1592.

Millay, Edna St. Vincent. *The Harp-Weaver and Other Poems*. New York, 1923.

Montesquieu, Charles Louis de. *L'Esprit des Lois*. 2 vols. Paris, 1748.

Motley, John L. *The Rise of the Dutch Republic*. 3 vols. Philadelphia, n.d.

Murray, Gilbert. *Five Stages of Greek Religion*. Oxford, 1925.

———. *The Ordeal of this Generation*. New York, 1929.

Noordhoff, L. J. *Beschrijving van het zich in Nederland bevindende en nog onbeschreven gedeelte der papieren afkomstig van Huig de Groot welke in 1864 te 's-Gravenhage zijn geveild*. Groningen, 1953.

Nys, Ernest. *Le Droit de la Guerre et les Précurseurs de Grotius*. Bruxelles, 1882.

Ottenwälder, Paul. *Zur Naturrechtslehre des Hugo Grotius*. Tübingen, 1950.

Pliny. *Letters*. Translated by William Melmouth. Vol. I. Cambridge, Mass., 1915. [Loeb's Classical Library.]

———. *Plinius Epistulae*. Edited by Selatie E. Stout. Bloomington, Ind., 1962.

Plutarch. *Plutarch's Moralia*. English translation by Frank C. Babbitt. Vol. IV. Cambridge, Mass., 1936. [Loeb's Classical Library.]

Pound, Roscoe. *The Formative Era of American Law*. Boston, 1938.

———. *The Lawyer from Antiquity to Modern Times*. St. Paul, Minn., 1953.

———. *Readings in Roman Law*. 2nd ed. Cambridge, Mass., 1914.

Ripperda-Wierdsma, Jan V. *Politie en Justitie: een studie over Hollandschen Staatsbouw tijdens de Republiek*. Zwolle, 1937.

Roldanus, Cornelia W. *Hugo de Groot's Bewijs van den waren Godsdienst*. Arnhem, 1944.

Schlüter, Joachim. *Die Theologie des Hugo Grotius*. Göttingen, 1919.

Seneca. *Seneca's Tragedies*. English translation by Frank J. Miller. Vol. I. New York, 1917. [Loeb's Classical Library.]

Sereni, Angelo P. *The Italian Conception of International Law*. New York, 1943.

Stubbs, William. *Seventeen Lectures on the Study of Medieval and Modern History*. 3rd ed. Oxford, 1900.

Vaillant, Christiaan. *Disputatio Juridica Exhibens Interpretationem Locorum Quorumdam Juris in Hugonis Grotii Epistolis*. Amsterdam, 1834.

Verdross, Alfred. *Die Verfassung der Völkerrechtsgemeinschaft*. Wien, 1926.

———. *Völkerrecht*. Berlin, 1937.

van Vollenhoven, Cornelis. *The Framework of Grotius' Book De Iure Belli ac Pacis* (1625). Amsterdam, 1932. [An excellent analysis of Grotius' best-known work.]

———. *De Jure Pacis*. The Hague, 1932.

———. *Verspreide Geschriften*. 3 vols. Haarlem, 1934. [Volume I contains numerous valuable articles on Grotius in English, French, and Dutch.]

de Vrankrijker, A. C. J. *De staatsleer van Hugo de Groot en zijn Nederlandsche tijdgenooten.* n.p. 1937.

Vreeland, Hamilton. *Hugo Grotius, the Father of the Modern Science of International Law.* New York, 1917.

Wehberg, Hans. *Hugo Grotius.* Wiesbaden, 1956.

Westermann, J. C. *The Netherlands and the United States.* The Hague, 1935.

van Wijk, F. W. *De republiek en Amerika, 1776–1782.* Leyden, 1921.

Wolff, Hans J. *Roman Law: An Historical Introduction.* Norman, 1951.

Wroth, L. Kinvin, and Hiller B. Zobel. *Legal Papers of John Adams.* 3 vols. Cambridge, Mass., 1965.

ARTICLES

Basdevant, Jules. "Étude sur quelques Pratiques du Droit des Gens à la Fin du XVIe Siècle et au Commencement du XVIIe, d'après les 'Annales' et 'Histoires' de Grotius," *Revue générale de Droit international public,* Vol. X (Sept.–Oct., 1903), 619–50.

Bodkin, E. H. "The *Adamus Exul* of Hugo Grotius," *Grotiana,* Vol. IV (1931), 17–35.

———. "The Minor Poetry of Hugo Grotius," *Transactions of the Grotius Society,* Vol. XIII (1928), 95–128.

Chafee, Zechariah, Jr. "Colonial Courts and the Common Law," *Proceedings* of the Massachusetts Historical Society, Vol. LXVIII (1952), 132–59.

Cleveringa, R. P. "B. M. Telders † 6 April 1945," *De Gids,* Vol. CVIII, No. 11 (Nov., 1945), 4–67.

Dovring, Folke. "Nouvelles recherches sur la Bibliothèque de Grotius en Suède et en Italie," *Mededeelingen der*

Koninklijken Nederlandsche Akademie van Weten-schappen, Afdeeling Letterkunde, nieuwe reeks, Vol. XIV, No. 10 (1951), 331–38.

——. "Une partie de l'héritage littéraire de Grotius re-trouvée en Suède," *Mededeelingen der Koninklijken Nederlandsche Akademie van Wetenschappen, Afdeeling Letterkunde,* nieuwe reeks, Vol. XII, No. 3 (1949), 237–50.

Dumbauld, Edward. "The *Florum Sparsio ad Jus Justin-ianeum* of Hugo Grotius," *Journal of Public Law,* Vol. XIV, No. 2 (Fall, 1965), 359–76.

——. "Grotius on the Law of Prize," *Journal of Public Law,* Vol. I, No. 2 (Fall, 1952), 370–89.

——. "Grotius' Defence of the Lawful Government of Holland," *Journal of Public Law,* Vol. III, No. 1 (Spring, 1954), 192–213.

——. "Grotius' Introduction to the Jurisprudence of Hol-land," *Journal of Public Law,* Vol. II, No. 1 (Spring, 1953), 112–27.

——. "Hugo Grotius: The Father of International Law," *Journal of Public Law,* Vol. I, No. 1 (Spring, 1952), 117–37.

——. "Judicial Review and Popular Sovereignty," *Uni-versity of Pennsylvania Law Review,* Vol. XCIX, No. 2 (Nov. 1950), 197–210.

——. "The Place of the Lawyer in International Affairs," address to the Fayette County Bar Association, February 4, 1933. *Uniontown, Pa., Morning Herald* (Feb. 6, 1933).

——. The Place of Philosophy in International Law," *University of Pennsylvania Law Review,* Vol. LXXXIII, No. 5 (Mar., 1935), 590–606.

———. "Thomas Jefferson and American Constitutional Law," *Journal of Public Law*, Vol. II, No. 2 (Fall, 1953), 370–89.

van Eysinga, Willem J. M. "De beteekenis van de Groot voor het internationale recht," *De Gids*, Vol. CVIII, No. 11 (Nov., 1945), 76–92. [Reprinted in *Sparsa Collecta*, 358–73.]

———. "Grotius (1625–1925)," *Revue de Droit international et de Législation comparée*, Vol. LII, No. 3 (1925), 269–79. [Reprinted in *Sparsa Collecta*, 123–30.]

———. "Grotius et la Chine," *Grotiana*, Vol. VII (1939), 20–27. [Reprinted in *Sparsa Collecta*, 255–64.]

———. "Het oudste bekende geschrift van de Groot over Volkenrecht," *Mededeelingen der Nederlandsche Akademie van Wetenschappen, Afdeeling Letterkunde, nieuwe reeks*, Vol. IV, No. 11 (1941), 463–72. [See *Sparsa Collecta*, 323–24.]

———. "Iets over de Groots Jongelingsjaren," *De Gids*, Vol. CV, No. 10 (Oct., 1941), 36–67.

———. "Quelques Observations au sujet du Mare Liberum et du De Iure Praedae de Grotius," *Grotiana*, Vol. IX (1942), 61–75. [Reprinted in *Sparsa Collecta*, 324–35.]

———. "Quelques observations sur Grotius et le droit romain," *Grotiana*, Vol. X (1947), 18–28. [Reprinted in *Sparsa Collecta*, 373–81.]

Fenwick, Charles G. "The Authority of Vattel," *American Political Science Review*, Vol. VII, No. 3 (Aug., 1913), 395–410.

Fockema-Andreae, S. J. "Une Étude de Droit comparé par Grotius," *Grotiana*, Vol. X (1947), 28–44.

Fruin, Robert J. "Geschiedenis der Inleiding tot de Hollandsche Rechts-geleerdheid, gedurende het leven des auteurs," in *Verspreide Geschriften*, VIII, 10–31. [First appeared in Fockema Andreae's 1895 edition of the *Inleiding*.)

———. "Hugo de Groot en Maria van Reigersbergh," *De Gids*, Vol. XXII–2 (Sept., 1858), 289–324; (Oct., 1858), 417–73. [Reprinted in *Verspreide Geschriften*, IV, 1–94.]

———. "Een onuitgegeven werk van Hugo de Groot," *De Gids*, Vol. XXXII–4 (Oct., 1868), 1–37; (Nov., 1868), 215–54. [Reprinted in Fruin's *Verspreide Geschriften*, III, 367–445.]

———. "An Unpublished Work of Hugo Grotius's," *Bibliotheca Visseriana*, Vol. V (1925), 3–74. [This is a translation of "Een onuitgegeven werk van Hugo de Groot," above.]

Hall, Ford W. "The Common Law: An Account of Its Reception in the United States," *Vanderbilt Law Review*, Vol. IV, No. 4 (June, 1951), 791–825.

Heijden, E. J. J. van der. "De Boekerij van Grotius," *Grotiana*, Vol. III (1930), 18–38.

Huizinga, J[ohan]. "Hugo de Groot en zijn eeuw," *De Gids*, Vol. LXXXIX, No. 7 (July, 1925), 1–16.

Jackson, Robert H. "Lawyers Today: The Legal Profession in a World of Paradox," *American Bar Association Journal*, Vol. XXXIII, No. 1 (Jan., 1947), 24–27, 85–89.

———. "Some Problems in Developing an International Legal System," *Temple Law Quarterly*, Vol. XXII, No. 2 (Oct., 1948), 147–58.

Kunz, Josef L. Book review [of Schätzel (editor and translator), *Hugo Grotius, De Jure Belli ac Pacis Libri Tres*], *American Journal of International Law*, Vol. XLV, No. 3 (July, 1951), 609–10.

Lauterpacht, Hersh. "The Grotian Tradition in International Law," *British Yearbook of International Law*, Vol. XXIII (1946), 1–53.

Meijers, E. M. "Boeken uit de bibliotheek van de Groot in de Universiteitsbibliotheek te Leiden," *Mededeelingen der Koninklijken Nederlandsche Akademie van Wetenschappen, Afdeeling Letterkunde*, nieuwe reeks, Vol. XII, No. 3 (1949), 251–79.

Molhuysen, Philip C. "De bibliotheek van Hugo de Groot in 1618," *Mededeelingen der Nederlandsche Akademie van Wetenschappen, Afdeeling Letterkunde*, nieuwe reeks, Vol. VI, No. 3 (1943), 45–63.

———. "The First Edition of Grotius's De Jure Belli ac Pacis," *Bibliotheca Visseriana*, Vol. V (1925), 103–49.

———. "Over de editio princeps van Grotius' De Iure Belli ac Pacis," *Mededeelingen der Koninklijke Akademie van Wetenschappen, Afdeeling Letterkunde*, Vol. LX, Series B, No. 1 (1925), 1–8.

———. "Over Grotius' De Jure Praedae Commentarius," *Bijdragen voor Vaderlandsche Geschiedenis en Oudheidkunde*, 6th Series, Vol. IV (1926), 275–82.

Moll, G. "De confiscatie der goederen van Hugo de Groot," *Oud-Holland*, Vol. XX, (1902), 83–112.

Nussbaum, Arthur. "Just War—A Legal Concept?," *Michigan Law Review*, Vol. XLII, No. 3 (Dec., 1943), 453–79.

Overdiep, G. S. "Hugo de Groot en onze nationale renaissance," *De Gids*, Vol. CIII-1, No. 2 (Feb., 1939), 188–208.

Pound, Roscoe. "Grotius in the Science of Law," *American Journal of International Law*, Vol. XIX, No. 4 (Oct., 1925), 685–88.

———. "Liberty of Contract," *Yale Law Journal*, Vol. XVIII, No. 7 (May, 1909), 454–87.

———. "Philosophical Theory and International Law," *Bibliotheca Visseriana*, Vol. I (1923), 73–90.

Reeves, Jesse. "The First Edition of Grotius' De Jure Belli ac Pacis, 1625," *American Journal of International Law*, Vol. XIX, No. 1 (Jan., 1925), 12–32.

———. "Grotius, De Jure Belli ac Pacis: A Bibliographical Account," *American Journal of International Law*, Vol. XIX, No. 2 (Apr., 1925), 251–62.

———. "The Life and Work of Hugo Grotius," *Proceedings* of the American Society of International Law, 48–58 (1925).

Rice, Harriet L. "The Unveiling of the Grotius Window at Delft," in *In the Carillon Country* (Ithaca, N. Y., 1933), 51–83.

Rivier, Alphonse. "La Mort de Grotius (28 août 1645)," *Revue de Droit international et de Législation comparée*, Vol. XIX, No. 1 (1887), 97–101.

Rogge, H[endrik] C. "De 'Verantwoordingh' van Hugo de Groot," *Bijdragen voor Vaderlandsche Geschiedenis en Oudheidkunde*, derde reeks, Vol. VII (1892), 89–134.

———. "Hugo de Groot te Parijs van 1621 tot 1625," *De Gids*, Vol. LVII (Aug., 1893), 249–73; (Sept., 1893), 450–77.

———. "Hugo de Groot's denkbeelden over de hereeniging der kerken," *Teyler's Theologisch Tijdschrift*, Vol. II, No. 1 (1904), 1–52.

Roldanus, Cornelia W. "De Groot als Theoloog," *De Gids*, Vol. CVIII, No. 12 (Dec., 1945), 103–25.

Sandifer, Durward V. "Rereading Grotius in the Year 1940," *American Journal of International Law*, Vol. XXXIV, No. 3 (July, 1940), 459–72.

Vissering, S. "De rechts-taal van H. de Groot's Inleiding tot de Hollandsche rechts-geleertheid," *Verslagen en Mededeelingen der Koninklijke Akademie van Wetenschappen, Afdeeling Letterkunde,* tweede reeks, Vol. XII (1883), 372–441.

van Vollenhoven, Cornelis. "On the Genesis of De Iure Belli ac Pacis (Grotius, 1625)," *Mededeelingen der Koninklijke Akademie van Wetenschappen, Afdeeling Letterkunde,* Series B, Vol. LVIII, No. 6 (1924), 125–55.

———. "The Growth of Grotius' De Iure Belli ac Pacis as It Appears from Contemporary Correspondence," *Bibliotheca Visseriana,* Vol. VI (1926), 131–77. Revised text, Vol. VIII (1929), 105–70, and reprinted in *Verspreide Geschriften,* I, 501–60.

Waterman, Julian S. "Thomas Jefferson and Blackstone's Commentaries," *Illinois Law Review,* Vol. XXVII, No. 6 (Feb., 1933), 629–59.

Weigert, Roger-Armand. "Les demeures de Grotius à Paris (1621–1645)," *Bulletin de la Société de l'Histoire du Protestantisme français,* Vol. XX (June–July, 1946), 137–51.

Wellschmied, Karl. "Zur Entstehung und Bedeutung der Inleidinge tot de Hollandsche Rechts-geleerheid von Hugo Grotius," *Zeitschrift der Savigny-Stiftung für Rechtsgeschichte, Germanischer Abteilung,* Vol. LXIX (1952), 155–81.

Wright, Herbert P. "Some Lesser Known Works of Hugo Grotius," *Bibliotheca Visseriana,* Vol. VII (1928), 131–238.

BIBLIOGRAPHY

INDEX

201

THE LIFE AND LEGAL WRITINGS OF HUGO GROTIUS was set on the Linotype in ten-point Electra, an American typeface designed by W. A. Dwiggins (1880–1956) and noted for its crisp calligraphic quality.

Display type is Janson, selected for its close resemblance to Dutch types in the days of Grotius, and the ornamental headpieces at the chapter openings are Linotype borders designed directly from seventeenth-century Dutch models.

The paper on which this book is printed bears the watermark of the University of Oklahoma Press and has an intended effective life of three hundred years.

UNIVERSITY OF OKLAHOMA PRESS

NORMAN